THE AUTHENTIC YOU: Becoming the Woman You Were Created to Be

Anita C. Lee

"With warmth and candor, Anita leads her readers on a great adventure—discovering who God means for them to be. This book will change lives!"

**Florence Littauer, best-selling author,
international speaker,
Founder of CLASSeminars; www.classeminars.org**

"Anita Lee has written the kind of book I love to read. Books about purpose and self discovery—Christian that is. The more I have delved into the understanding of just who I am and why I am here, the more focused I have become. A Choleric and a 'bottom-line' woman, I love facts. The more the better. I can't wait to get my hands on Anita's entire book. I can tell I am about to discover more about myself—Anita Lee style!"

**Ann Platz, author, speaker, designer from Atlanta, Ga
www.AnnPlatz.com**

"As a seasoned therapist who has spent years helping women move out of bondage and into the loving light of Jesus I wholeheartedly recommend my friend Anita Lee's book, *The Authentic You*. Anita combines the seasoning of the wise older woman that Paul talks about in Scripture, with a dynamic process that is designed to take a woman on a journey inward to discover her true God-given worth, value, and dreams. Anita then takes the reader on the outward journey to re-engage an intentional, hope-filled, spirit-led life. Her practical, biblical approach will empower the women who read and study this resource."

John H. Thurman Jr. M.Div., M.A., (LCMHC) Licensed Clinical Mental Health Counselor, BCPCC (Board Certified Professional Christian Counselor)

"With honesty and openness, Anita Lee sets out a clear path that will lead you to the discovery of all that God intends for your life. Anita gives practical instructions to help you find your authentic self and live a fulfilled, purposeful life. She shares her own story, and her credibility speaks. This is a book to read and reread, and to give to others."

Betty Southard, Spiritual Director, CLASSeminars Trainer, Speaker, Author of *Come As You Are, The Mentor Quest* **and** *The Grandmother Book.*

"Authenticity is one of today's buzz words. Why? Because as a society we want evidence of what is real in this generation. This is a high expectation! Therefore, we should be compelled to have it start with us! This book is a must read for any woman who seeks to be "authentic"—ultimately impacting her present spheres of influence and the next generation of women!"

Doreen Hanna, President/Founder of Treasured Celebrations Ministries
Co-author of *Raising a Modern Day Princess*
CLASSeminars Faculty Speaker
www.doreenhanna.org

"In an age when women still need permission to be real, in spite of women's liberation, *The Authentic You* opens the way for truth that validates and sets us free. I'm recommending this book to all the single moms that carry the question, 'Who am I, really?'"

Gail Cawley Showalter, Founder of SMORE for Women—Single Moms - Overjoyed, Rejuvenated, Empowered!
www.smoreforwomen.org

"It thrills my spirit to imagine the women who can bask in a new kind of freedom because of the words in this book. I'm not only excited about the action steps that Anita provides, but also about this whole new vision for living!"

Kathi Lipp, national speaker
author of *The Husband Project*
www.KathiLipp.com

"If there is ever a need for authenticity it is now! Anita coaches us to authentic living in every area of our life and then asks the ultimate question, 'Who is looking to you for direction in life?' "

Linda Olson, Founder of Made for Something More,
professional speaker
Author of *Exceeding Your Expectations*
www.madeforsomethingmore.com

"The time for this book is NOW. Anita's message pierced the noise of my busy schedule with its clarity and gentleness. This book will cause you to take notice of key issues keeping you from stepping into the destiny that God intends for you."

Rosemary Hossenlopp, MBA
Author of *Step Into Your Future*
www.ChristianBizWoman.com

"Authenticity, in a simple, wrap your hands around it concept, is what Anita Lee delivers in her book, *The Authentic You*. Every generation of women can benefit from the freedom-filled words you find throughout her book. Really getting, 'If she had fully embraced her life as a woman created in perfection by God, Satan's temptation would have been powerless over her (Eve)' breaks the bounds of disillusionment that keep so many of us powerlessly tied to lies of the past. The way we reach beyond the world's lies is by being real. *The Authentic You* gives us the tools to become just that."

Linda Goldfarb - The Power Lady
Founder of Live Powerfully Now Ministries
Speaker, E-TV/Talk Radio Host, and writer
www.LivePowerfullyNow.org

THE AUTHENTIC YOU:
Becoming the Woman You Were Created to Be

Anita C. Lee

Copyright © 2010 by Anita C. Lee

All rights reserved.

ISBN: 1453778268
ISBN-13: 9781453778265

Unless otherwise identified, all scripture quotations in this publication are taken from the HOLY BIBLE, NEW INTERNATIONAL VERSION. Copyright© 1973, 1978, 1984 International Bible Society. Used by permission of Zondervan Bible Publishers.

Scripture notated (THE MESSAGE) is taken from THE MESSAGE. Copyright© 1993, 1994, 1995, 1996, 2000, 2001, 2002. Used by permission of NavPress Publishing Group.

Scripture notated (NRSV) is from the New Revised Standard Version Bible, copyright 1989, by the Division of Christian Education of the National Council of the Churches of Christ in the U.S.A. Used by permission. All rights reserved.

Dedication

To Abby and Lily, who teach me new life lessons each day.
I pray that you will become Godly women following in your
mother's footsteps.

Contents

Introduction XV
Invitation to Authenticity

Chapter One 1
Authentic Questioning: Discovering who you are and why it matters

Chapter Two 25
Authentic Listening: Identifying where you are in life and where you want to be

Chapter Three 45
Authentic Bearing: Standing tall with confidence—going beyond self-esteem to God's esteem

Chapter Four 61
Authentic Forgiving: Offering forgiveness and grace—Accepting forgiveness and grace

Chapter Five 79
Authentic Growing: Moving from mediocre to marvelous

Chapter Six 97
Authentic Dreaming: Learning to dream again—asking God for the vision

Chapter Seven 115
Authentic Trusting: Taking faith steps—trusting God for the future

Chapter Eight 131
Authentic Planning: Embracing the courage to change step by step

Chapter Nine 145
Authentic Living: Experiencing life according to God's plan

Chapter Ten 159
Authentic Leading: Becoming a beacon to those around you

A Message from the Author 175

About the Author 177

Acknowledgements

Unending thanks to Daryl, who believed in me and my gifts long before I could believe for myself. I'm grateful for how you support me in every way imaginable.

Also deep thanks to Meredith, who has taught me patience and acceptance (she's a much better mother than I); to Adam, who opens my eyes to a wider world of creativity; and to other family members and friends who have greatly impacted my life.

I have had many mentors over the years who have encouraged me to step out of my comfort zone and do more than I thought possible. Special thanks to Drs. Britton and Bobbye Wood and to Rev. Ellen Shepard.

A warm tribute to the dynamic people of CLASSeminars for imparting knowledge and instilling confidence as I pursued writing and speaking. I commend all my "CLASSmates" who have shared their experiences and wisdom unselfishly with men and women throughout the world.

This book was helped immensely by intrepid readers who volunteered to read the early manuscript and give needed feedback. I appreciate each of you for making this a better book than it would have been without you.

I thank my coaches, Sheryl Stewart and Jane Emberty, for spurring me on to do the things I felt called to do. (Yes, life coaches have coaches, too!) Also thanks go to my coaching clients and seminar participants, past and present, who boldly take the challenge to dream big dreams and live them out. I am honored and privileged to share in your lives.

My greatest thanks and praise go to the Creator God who knows us completely and even so, loves us unconditionally.

Introduction:
Your Invitation to Authenticity

WHEN YOU HAVE OBSERVED THE WORLD and its people as long as I have, you learn a few things. One discovery I've made is that we can never be fully at peace with ourselves if we don't come to terms with who we are and who God has created us to be. If those two things are in conflict, our whole being is out of balance.

This book is meant to be a heart-to-heart visit between you and me. It is from one who has experienced the pain of a lost identity, to the woman who is hurting today as she tries to find herself. It is a friend-to-friend book, perhaps a mentor-to-protégé book. And although there are several excellent volumes dealing with authenticity—some written by psychologists, religious leaders or other professionals—this one is especially for you today.

We were created to live rich fulfilling lives. Yet, so often I talk to women who are just going through the motions, taking life as it comes rather than living intentionally.

My prayer is that if you are feeling lost in a jumble of responsibilities, expectations and false identities, you will draw something from these pages that will give you courage to do the hard work of discovering the woman God created you to be for this phase of your life. It may involve giving up the guilt of past mistakes, learning to forgive others (and yourself) and staring down your fear of the future.

It might take weeks or months to get to the place you need to be. It could very well be difficult and heart-wrenching. It will certainly be worthwhile, if you persevere with God's help to let go of the person you've been trying to be, in order to become the authentic person you were created to be.

So, grab a cup of coffee or tea, curl up in a comfortable chair and come along on the journey.

Chapter One
Authentic Questioning: Discovering *who* you are and why it matters

"O LORD, YOU HAVE SEARCHED ME and you know me... For you created my inmost being; you knit me together in my mother's womb. I praise you because I am fearfully and wonderfully made; your works are wonderful, I know that full well."

Psalm 139:1, 13, 14

> *The young woman made her way quickly to the front of the chapel at the end of the worship service. She grabbed the hand of one of the Christian counselors who stood waiting to pray for those with special requests. Between her sobs she poured out the words that summed up her struggle:* "I don't know who I am."

Many women, Christian and non-Christian alike, could take that young woman's place. A look at magazine headlines, song lyrics and self-help books suggests that we are busier than ever, have more "toys" than ever, but may be more lost than ever. We seldom take the time to examine our lives to really know our true identities—our authentic selves—and the lives for which God created us.

Maybe that's where you are today. If you cannot look at yourself in the mirror and pronounce, "I am fearfully and wonderfully made—made to do incredible things," you are not saying about yourself what God says, and you are not thinking what God thinks about you. You do not know your true self.

Not knowing ourselves or feeling that we have to play a game of pretense can pull us down in a daily struggle, as we try to be someone we're not. The energy drain is costly as we compare ourselves with those around us—or even worse, with the airbrushed photos of media figures gracing the front of women's magazines.

How did we come to this state of affairs? As early as the 5th century B.C., Socrates is said to have admonished his followers, "Know thyself." And he probably wasn't the first to suggest this. Yet many of us are no closer to that essential knowledge than were the early Greeks.

For decades, my friend Sherry and I lamented that we didn't know what we wanted to be when we grew up. We laughed about it, but secretly I wondered if there was something different I should be doing. Maybe I was missing my calling, not taking advantage of my opportunities.

As our opportunities expand today, so do our responsibilities. A fulltime job in addition to keeping a household is considered normal today. Add a husband and children to the mix and you have a recipe for overload.

Yes, there's opportunity out there, yet so often our responsibilities seem to keep us from pursuing our dreams. We fear we may be missing out on something, but don't see how we could move from where we are to where we'd like to be—to become our true selves.

"Who am I? I'll tell you who I am. I'm a wife and mother and daughter of ill, elderly parents and an employee and a community volunteer and …"

We can rattle off a litany of responsibilities, many of them unknown to former generations. Have you ever looked back at your grandmother's life and envied the seeming simplicity of that era?

You *are* what you *do*. Or are you?
Wasn't women's lib supposed to take care of this dilemma of not knowing ourselves? When women in the 1970's traded the diaper-changing table for the boardroom table, many thought they would be the first generation able to embrace their true identities. They would be unencumbered by preconceived ideas about who they should become—of what society had expected of their gender. Barriers were broken and women moved into areas unknown to them in the past.

Yet we're still asking the same questions. "Is this the person I most want to be?" "Am I being true to myself?" And for the committed Christian, "Is this who God wants me to be?"

It's simply part of the human experience to question our significance, and it's necessary for continual growth. Whether you are a stay-at-home mom or a corporate executive, it's a good idea to reassess and re-evaluate your life periodically to see if you're in the right place for your life stage. Being the true *you* may look very different at different times in your life.

To "work" or not to "work"—what kind of question is that?

All women may be created equal, but they're not alike and their approaches to living will vary with their needs and circumstances. The decision whether or not to work outside the home has been hotly debated in Christian circles, with Godly women coming down on all sides of the argument.

For some women the thought of staying home and not having a job is equivalent to wasting their God-given talents. After prayer and soul-searching they have concluded that they are in the center of God's will as they work outside the home and enjoy a healthy family life, too.

Women often move into and out of corporate life at various times throughout their working years. Yes, there are sacrifices when a woman leaves the working world to stay at home for a season. If she re-enters the workforce later she may very well find herself at a lower rung on the ladder than if she had stayed. But many women recognize this and choose to embrace motherhood as a fulltime job for awhile.

Other women have chosen both career and family, but haven't done very well on the family side. These women may believe they have been good role-models for the next generation of women. However, some of their daughters are not impressed and have chosen to stay at home with their own children.

There are SAHMS (Stay at Home Moms) who were born for this job. This mom loves having little ones around (and may be sad to see them grow up and become independent). She breezes through the work that needs to be done around the house or is able to ignore the undone chores, knowing they will wait until another day.

Additionally, there are SAHMs who do not feel very successful being at home. Sometimes depression causes this mom to go into a tailspin, staring at walls that seem to be closing in on her and feeling guilty that she is not doing the laundry or other household chores.

There are no easy answers to what a Christian woman's role should be. And certainly there are no one-size-fits-all solutions. However, knowing how God has gifted us and understanding our strengths and weaknesses can help us make wise decisions. Being open to changes throughout life also prepares us to accept the challenge to become more than we are now and to live abundantly.

Later in this chapter we will explore personalities and temperaments to help us understand why we're the way we are and learn how to develop the positive aspects of our personalities.

Life purpose—a relatively new and narrow phenomenon?
Today there is a guilt-inducing, almost pathological search among some people to find their passion, their *one* true calling in life. The hunt is often associated with trying to find the right job. We've gone from "Bloom where you're planted" to "Plant yourself where you can bloom." We long for work that is fulfilling to the depths of our souls, not just time-filling or wealth-giving. This concentration on doing work that meets our deepest needs is a relatively new twist for women and even today is not shared by women in many other parts of the world.

What were the choices for my mother and her mother before her? My grandmother may have been happy or unhappy from one day to the next, but because there was cotton to pick, water to haul from the well and clothes to boil clean, she probably didn't spend much time wondering if she should seek more fulfilling work. However, she found gratification in canning vegetables from the kitchen garden, crocheting doll clothes for her five granddaughters and quilting with her friends from the church and community.

Life was physically easier for my mother than for my grandmother. My mother lived in a city, drove a car, owned a washer and dryer and worked outside the home after her youngest child entered school. Her choices were far greater than for the generation before her. She worked to help support her parents in their declining years, probably without suffering stigma from her friends in the community, as many of them also held jobs.

By the time I graduated from college the world was limitless—or at least it seemed so to me. One opportunity I treasure was being able to live abroad. Two years living and teaching in Japan as that society was making rapid social changes helped me to see how drastically life can change in a short time. While there, in the late 1960's, I met several young people and enjoyed learning more about the Japanese culture from them as they practiced their English skills on me. A young lady told me one day that she was getting married and would not be able to visit with me any longer. I congratulated her.

"It is the end of my life," was her sad reply.

I was stunned. Then I learned that almost all of the girls I knew would end up in arranged marriages, with the parents deciding who they would marry. "Love marriages" were not unheard of, but neither were they common among those I met in the 1960's.

This wider view of the world gave me experiences my foremothers scarcely could have dreamed of. I also saw firsthand that in some other parts of the world life had not changed much from generation to generation. And I gained a new sense of responsibility for the opportunities before me.

When our children were young, during the 1980s, my husband and I taught for a year at a university in the People's Republic of China. One of our family's favorite Sunday afternoon pastimes was to walk in the nearby countryside. We were always greeted by several of the local children practicing their "Hah-lo's" and "Gooood-bye's." Feeling like Pied Pipers, we would lead a parade of giggling children through the grain fields. Several simple adobe-style houses, some topped with thatch, others modernized with blue tile roofs, stood in a clearing nearby. Chickens pecked for grain in the packed-dirt courtyards and scurried into and out of houses at will. When we walked by, the old people would greet us: *"Chi fan le ma?" –Have you eaten yet?* It was the accustomed greeting in a country that had had an ongoing and even recent history of famine.

I doubt that those farmwives in China woke up every morning and asked themselves if they were feeling fulfilled, if this was their true purpose in life. There was too much work to do to indulge in such frivolity. However, their daughters may very well have choices that allow them to ask such questions.

Choices today

Our choices today in the United States do seem endless. Because we have the luxury of choosing among a staggering number of ways to fill our time, it can be overpowering.

Counselor and author Richard Leider says: "People are intimidated by how much choice they have. There are almost too many career choices, too many life choices. People are overwhelmed at times by the decisions they get to make—and have to make—about their jobs, their families, their businesses, their futures...If you don't have a way to sort it all out, you can become paralyzed."[1]

So we try to narrow the choices by examining what we are passionate about—what our one true calling is. But as I see it, it's not always a matter of finding the one true passion in our lives that will stay the same forever and ever. Instead, it's essential that we examine our gifts and abilities and seek God's will for our lives today and again tomorrow and all the tomorrows allotted us.

It is our responsibility to look at the possibilities and make the most of our lives by living authentically—as God intended for us—and through that authenticity to reach out to others.

What keeps you from being authentic?

There are numerous reasons why a woman might choose to play a role rather than do the hard work of discovering and living out her true identity. Do you struggle with knowing who you are or who you could be? Have you fallen into a role out of necessity but find you are ready to move on—if you just knew how to do it?

Laurie Beth Jones, in her book, *Jesus: Life Coach*, says, "Never before in the history of the world has a civilization been more capable of living fully expressed and developed lives, yet the statistics are still staggering that we are not."[2]

---

[1] Alan M. Webber, "Are You Deciding On Purpose" (extended interview with Richard Leider), *Fast Company*, Issue 13, January 1998, p. 114.

[2] Laurie Beth Jones, *Jesus: Life Coach*, (Nashville, Tennessee: Thomas Nelson, 2004), 131.

We can remedy that problem when we consciously and perseveringly seek God's will for our lives. Part of the path in knowing God's will for your life is learning where your strengths and weaknesses lie, what your unique talents and gifts are and where you are in life's inventory of ages and stages.

Beware of identity fraud—understanding your personality

A study of personality or temperament differences helps us better understand ourselves and others. It also can point out the disconnect that comes when we negate our true nature and assume the traits of one of the other types. Books by Florence Littauer, Marita Littauer, Tim LaHaye and Beverly LaHaye introduced a Christian slant to the study of the four temperaments as described by Hippocrates, the early Greek doctor and philosopher.

Other personality profiles such as those by Isabel Briggs Myers and Katharine Cook Briggs (Myers-Briggs Type Indicator) and Dr. John Trent and Dr. Gary Smalley have been very helpful to individuals and corporations as participants learn how different personalities influence how we operate and how we relate to others.

Doing an on-line search for the word "temperament" or for "four basic personalities" will point you to information that, if used correctly, can be of great help in determining these traits in yourself. In some cases, profiles or assessments are available on-line.

All of these models have been used effectively in Christian pastoral care and coaching. In studying these systems, I have found them to be not only instructive for learning more about human behavior, but freeing, as I realize I am created differently from friends and family members. And while this does not give me an excuse to shirk duties, it does help me understand why I *naturally* am inclined in one direction or another.

What a relief to learn that God loves me just the way he made me—although he expects me to grow and mature spiritually, mentally and emotionally.

Not only has it helped me understand myself, it has helped immensely in understanding other people and accepting them for who they are, not who I would like for them to be!

The Personalities/Temperaments

If you are not familiar with any of the above mentioned systems, I encourage you to study one or more for a better understanding of yourself and those around you. It can greatly enhance your relationships at home, in the workplace and in your community of believers.

A brief description of the four basic personalities or temperaments can give us a framework to help us talk about our differences, even though it is a superficial or simplistic overview. Each person typically will exhibit characteristics of more than one type, in varying amounts.

"You are My Sunshine."—The Sanguine Personality

The Sanguine is noted for a cheery outlook and loves being the center of attention. She is the life of the party and may keep others in stitches telling stories—stories that may stretch the truth a bit but are highly entertaining. However, the sanguine person may have trouble keeping secrets or not sharing things that are better kept quiet.

"Get it done and get it done NOW."—The Choleric Personality

She's on a mission and she knows she's the one to do it so it will be done right. She wants to be appreciated for the work she does. And while she may be a bit too "in your face" for some people, she does get the job done.

"Let's have some order around here."—The Melancholy Personality

This is the gal in your office who has every paperclip lined up in her desk drawer, every pencil sharpened and her files actually *in* the filing cabinet. She needs order and structure in her life and may prefer being alone to get things done.

"Whatever."—The Phlegmatic

Although some have characterized the phlegmatic as lazy, this personality can be very productive—but usually at a slower pace than others. She needs peace and calm and will bring those attributes to the workplace or home.

Do you see yourself in one or more of these personalities? What about other family members or people you work with?

The challenge begins when people are placed together in families, workplaces, churches and communities. Not everyone thinks and reacts the same to circumstances. And we usually think others should do as we do. The joke at our house whenever we see something we don't agree with—whether done by someone in our family or some powerful world figure—is, "Why didn't they ask me? I could have told them the *right* way to do it."

As Marita Littauer points out in her book, *Wired That Way*, "We all have had situations with people in which we have tried everything we know how to do to get along with them, but nothing seems to work. No matter how hard we try we cannot change those individuals. However...we can change ourselves—we can grow and improve. We can also change our approach to others so that we can, so far as it depends on us, be at peace with everyone."[3]

---

3 Marita Littauer, *Wired That Way* (Ventura, California: Regal Books), 11-12.

Wearing a mask

Sometimes instead of operating out of our true personality, we cover that identity by adopting another. This is often done subconsciously and the one "wearing a mask" may not realize that it is happening.

Speaker and writer Carol R. Cool explains:

> I have had what can only be described as a blessed life. And yet a poster hanging on my office wall expresses what I have felt since childhood: "Masquerading as a normal person day after day is exhausting."
>
> Trying to fit in, to be like everyone else, to follow another's "correct" path, has often kept me from being the woman God created me to be and wanted to use. Now, as I speak and write on evangelism, social justice, balance and parenting, I try to help people discover and celebrate their own uniqueness so they don't waste the number of years I have, striving to be someone they were never meant to be.[4]

The fact is, nobody can be a better *you*, than *you*. But if you are hiding behind a façade that keeps people from knowing the real you, you are shortchanging yourself and those around you who could benefit from your gifts and abilities.

External and internal influences contribute to masking

(The following stories represent women of varying backgrounds and temperaments. The names have been changed to protect the privacy of

---

4   Carol Cool, personal correspondence with the author.

each. If you see yourself in any of these stories, this book is definitely for you!)

Lisa, who grew up in a dysfunctional family, learned early in life that the bubbly, outgoing person that she was by nature did not cut it at home. In order to keep peace and meet the expectations of her parents, Lisa put on a different face. She became subdued and serious.

Not until she was an adult and started studying personality and temperament differences, did Lisa realize there was a whole different person living inside her skin.

Julie was fairly outgoing and fun-loving throughout high school, but things changed when she met Keith in college. She thrived on the attention he gave her when they first met and considered it a demonstration of his deep love when he became jealous of her time spent with anyone else. He demanded that she not go out unless she was with him. Even a lunch date with "the girls" was not on his list of approved appointments. Julie soon changed from the life of the party to a solemn, melancholy individual. She became adept at subduing her natural emotions and interests in order to keep peace in her relationship with Keith. Marriage a few years later did not improve the situation.

For Denise, the problem was more internal. Her mother died when Denise and her sisters were very young. In some ways she felt a need to take her place, mothering her younger siblings with seriousness far beyond her years. Other adults had not expected her to fill this role, but Denise felt the need to do so. As an adult she recently learned to laugh and do silly things she had missed out on as a child.

Anna had yet a different problem. "As the middle child of working parents, I felt invisible and began clowning around to get attention. Although I really wasn't outgoing naturally, I looked around and saw that the kids who got attention at school and church were the ones who were loud and boisterous. I watched them carefully and mimicked their actions."

After awhile this behavior became a strain on Anna, as she tried to keep up the façade. "It was such a relief to just be myself," she explained later of her new-found, quieter personality.

Who is that masked lady?

Recognizing the masks we wear may take years of self-searching. It also might be necessary to have professional help in discarding the old self for the new, authentic one. No matter how you go about the work of unveiling the true person beneath the mask, know that God has a hand in the discovery path and stands ready to lift you to new places and a better understanding of yourself and his unconditional love for you.

Living in a time-warp

Sometimes we're caught in a time-warp of who we were supposed to be at one time. We have not moved on as life has changed around us. This can be detrimental to relationships and even to our jobs. A crippling fear hides behind the refusal to change and to learn new things, such as the technology necessary in many jobs today. We're afraid we won't be able to learn new skills, so we resist, insisting that the old way is better.

Years ago when I was a middle school teacher, our principal informed us that new technology made it possible for us to post daily grades into a computer program. Then at the end of the semester all the grades could be averaged, even weighting test grades differently from daily homework. Voila! In an instant our report card grades were done. This was a small miracle for me—the "I hate numbers" person. I was surprised at the reaction from one of the teachers on my team. She thought of all kinds of reasons this was not a good idea. *The grades might get lost. It takes too much time. I like doing it the way I've always done it.* But when I questioned her further, I discovered that she was uncomfortable using computers. She was afraid she would be a failure at it and look like a fool.

Another way we try to hold on to the person we used to be, instead of moving into new phases of life, is by not letting go of our children. Perhaps you've seen parents who never move from being the authoritarian figure to being a friend to their adult children. Yes, the Bible says children should obey their parents, but it also says that parents should not exasperate their children. As our children move to adulthood, our roles as parents change. By encouraging our young adults to grow and mature spiritually we help them in their own quests to become who God created them to be.

Life means change. Period. How can we embrace needed change and still be true to who we really are—or who we need to become?

Spiritual need, not vocational

"Today's challenge is to lead an examined life in an unexamining age," says Os Guinness in his book, *Long Journey Home: A Guide to Your Search for the Meaning of Life.*[5]

Part of the problem lies in not asking the right questions. We look for a job that is fulfilling or we sign on to volunteer in the community, expecting those activities to fulfill our personal

---

5   Os Guinness, *Long Journey Home: A Guide to Your Search for the Meaning of Life* (Nashville, W Publishing Group, 2003), 12.

need. Instead we find we have filled hours but not the longing in our hearts. The reality may be that we're trying to fill a spiritual void with activities that, although worthy and helpful to others, do not meet our soul need.

Fed by our desires, hopes and dreams, we want more than a mundane existence. Yet we can waste time and energy if we don't realize ours is a spiritual odyssey.

So where do we go for answers?

Getting real in Christian groups

Often groups within the church are not any better at authentic living than those outside the church. It's not that they intend to be inauthentic, but they may be doing the best they can to hold life together, assuming that everyone else is OK, even when they are not. We all look pretty good on Sunday morning, sitting around in Bible study.

The loneliest time in my life was as a young mom when I was very active in a church, attended a couple of Bible studies each week and had many Christian friends. But in spite of often being among those Christian friends, I felt I could not confide that my life was falling apart. We all showed up at church and Bible studies well-dressed, smiling and bantering with one another. My pain was invisible. I remember sitting in a beautifully appointed living room at a mid-week Bible study and looking around the circle at the faces of those gathered. I was convinced I was the only one there who felt that life was a struggle.

It was only after getting a wake-up call that I was finally able to confide in a friend how miserable I was. Ironically I was on the way to church one day for yet another meeting, with my two toddlers strapped into their car-seats. As I stopped at a traffic light, feeling depressed and overwhelmed, my eyes focused on the overpass abutment just beyond the intersection. I thought wearily, *I could drive right into one of those pillars at high speed and no one would know it was done on purpose.* While I had no intention of doing so, the very fact that it had entered my mind got my attention. I knew I needed help. As soon as I got home I phoned a church friend who I knew had been through repeated difficulties. I didn't even know her very well, but all my other Christian friends seemed to have such perfect lives, I didn't feel like I could call them. I now believe God had directed me to call the right person.

Sarah was immediately supportive. "What have you eaten today?"

It seemed like a strange question, but I confessed I had not been eating very healthily. "Chocolate candy and potato chips."

"O.K., first thing you do is start eating properly. It could be affecting your mood."

Within a week of consuming a healthier diet, the fog lifted and I began to feel like my old self—able to roll with the punches.

And although I hadn't felt comfortable admitting my difficulties in the Bible study classes, it was through a Christian friend that I received help.

We could help one another by being honest. Transparency is a missing factor in some of our Christian groups, withholding the needed support that we could use. Do you need a friend who will listen non-judgmentally, will pray for you and will hold your problems in secret? Can you be such a friend to someone else? Look around you in the Christian groups you frequent to see if there is someone with whom you could have honest dialogue. Ask God to guide you to someone who can share your load or for whom you could be a load bearer.

NOTE: I was fortunate that a change in diet put me back on an even keel. However, such an easy solution is not always the answer. If you suffer from sadness or listlessness and can't seem to shake it, more help may be called for. God has gifted many professionals with the ability to assist people dealing with depression. Take advantage of those gifts to help you return to the life God would have you live.

Discovering our spiritual gifts

"Just as each of us has one body with many members, and these members do not all have the same function, so in Christ we who are many form one body, and each member belongs to all the others. We have different gifts, according to the grace given us. If a man's gift is prophesying, let him use it in proportion to his faith. If it is serving, let him serve; if it is teaching, let him teach; if it is encouraging, let him encourage; if it is contributing to the needs of others, let him give generously; if it is leadership, let him govern diligently; if it is showing mercy, let him do it cheerfully." Romans 12:4-8

Many books have been written about how to discover and use your spiritual gifts, yet not all Christians have explored this area of their lives. In his book, *S.H.A.P.E.: Finding & Fulfilling Your Unique Purpose for Life*, Erik Rees encourages readers to discover their own gifts and abilities. "God's purposes in our lives unfold as we open ourselves to his possibilities. We begin to see the shape of his masterpiece in our lives when we identify and focus on the passions he has placed in our hearts."[6]

---

6   Erik Rees, *S.H.A.P.E.: Finding & Fulfilling Your Unique Purpose for Life* (Grand Rapids, Michigan: Zondervan, 2006), 58.

We were in the home of new friends in Atlanta for dinner one evening when the subject of spiritual gifts came up. I would be teaching on the subject in Bible study the next Sunday morning and wanted to get our friends' input.

"Oh, I don't have any gifts," said the wife modestly as she served the delicious meal.

"I can't believe you said that!" I responded, surprised at her answer.

I couldn't let her denial pass without further comment, as I feel we need to recognize and use our gifts. I told her she probably had many gifts, but I was sure of at least one—the gift of hospitality. I had wanted to move in as soon as we entered the doors of their stunning home. But it was not just the beauty of the house that embraced us, it was the warmth and welcome of the occupants.

"Oh, this is just what I do easily," she countered.

Typically, we enjoy and "do easily" those things that we have been gifted to do. When I take gifts surveys, my score is appallingly low in the gift of helping (as well as many other gifts). Although I certainly want to help when called upon, I'm not likely to notice and volunteer for tasks that someone with the gift of *helping* sees. I'm more likely to step up to the plate when teaching or encouragement is needed.

Eric Rees notes 20 spiritual gifts taken from three places in the New Testament where the subject is mentioned. (1 Corinthians 12:28, Ephesians 4:11 and 1 Peter 4:9-10.) They are: administration, apostleship, discernment, encouragement, evangelism, faith, giving, healing, helping, hospitality, interpretation, knowledge, leadership, mercy, miracles, pastoring, prophecy, teaching, tongues and wisdom.

Just as with temperaments and personality traits, information and assessments of spiritual gifts can be found on-line.

Be judicious in using the information found through on-line searches, just as you would in using books on the subject. Look for credentials and credibility of those who have posted such information.

If I enjoy it, it must be wrong
Unfortunately, some Christians have gotten the idea that if we enjoy doing something, it must be wrong, that God calls us to turn from our natural interests and passions to "suffer for the faith."

Yes, we might need to give up an activity that gets in the way of our relationship with God—if we place anything before God it is an idol—but to refute the gifts God has given us is not piety, but rejection.

By tapping into our natural abilities, gifts, interests and talents, and seeking God's will in how to integrate all facets of ourselves for the Kingdom, we become co-laborers with God. We are called to take the good news of redemption and abundant life to a hurting world and are gifted to do that in an amazing variety of ways.

The same yesterday, today and tomorrow
Some things are constants no matter what your present role in life. These are truths we can depend on as we seek to know ourselves better: God is love. God never changes. God cares for us. God will lead us along the right path if we seek proper guidance.

But *we* may need to change. We may need to let go of previously held ideas of who we are and step out in faith that God can lead us to become who we were created to be for this time in our lives. It may be time to ask ourselves some questions about the stages we are in, whether single, married, or single-again.

God wants to use you to reach others—to be feet and hands and heart to love those around you.

Something to think about
When you get right down to it, wasn't Eve's problem in the garden that she didn't know or accept who she was? If she had fully embraced her life as a woman created in perfection by God, Satan's temptation would have been powerless over her.

We are all Eve. We look around for something better—and within God's leading we should always be looking for the best. We are created with a bent for living large unless fears have dampened that urge. But when we go our own way to find the answers, failing to put God first, we are in danger of leaving the garden for something less than what is best for us. When we give in to the pressures of society or friends or even family, rather than seeking God's face, we are in danger of becoming disconnected, frazzled and unsure of ourselves. We may well wonder, "Who am I?"

We find our answer in Ephesians 1:11. "It's in Christ that we find out who we are and what we are living for…" (THE MESSAGE)

Come along as we learn in the next chapters how to uncover our true selves, so we can live abundant lives, blessing others as we go.

ACTION STEPS:
Questions to help you know yourself better and to become a blessing to those around you—

Consider keeping a journal while working through this book and record your answers to these questions. Or you might prefer to just write your answers on a sheet of paper or index card so you can post it and read your answers regularly, to help you grow.

1. Do you know your personality/temperament type and your spiritual gifts?
2. If so, are you working in your strengths and using your gifts?
3. If not, will you take the time to investigate those and try to move toward exercising your gifts, talents and abilities?
4. Do you often feel 'disconnected' from your true self?
5. What positive step(s) could you take to move closer to becoming your true self?
6. What do you enjoy doing and have natural abilities to do?
7. What do others praise you for? (Even if you're in the habit of discounting their praise!)
8. What have you always wanted to learn?
9. What have you always wanted to try doing?
10. If you could do anything in life, what would you do?

After answering the above questions, see if there is a pattern that

> **Get to Know Yourself by Learning About Temperaments and Personalities:**
>
> *The New Spirit-Controlled Woman* by Beverly LaHaye. Harvest House Publishers.
>
> *Talk Easy, Listen Hard* by Nancy Sebastian Meyer. Moody Publishers.
>
> *The Two Sides of Love* by Gary Smalley and John Trent. Tyndale House Publishers.
>
> *Type Talk: The 16 Personality Types That Determine How We Live, Love, and Work* by Otto Kroeger and Janet M. Thuesen. Dell Publishing.
>
> *Wired That Way* by Marita Littauer with insights from Florence Littauer. Regal Books.

helps you understand yourself better. Even if some of your answers don't seem feasible for your life now, are there underlying ideas that could be incorporated into your present life? For example, if you always wanted to be an Olympic gymnast and that's not possible now, are there other related activities that are possible—helping Olympic hopefuls, doing workouts that use the same muscles as gymnastics, etc?

It can be helpful to work with an understanding friend or a life coach to move from where you are now to where you want to be in the future.

NOTE: Understanding your own personality can guide you in what kind of journal to use. I write more freely in an inexpensive notebook that I can comfortably hold in my lap. For the beautiful journals I continue to buy, but am afraid to write in because I might "mess them up," I record favorite quotes, scriptures and blessings I've received, rather than the untidy ramblings of my heart. You, however, could be the type who is encouraged by a beautiful journal or "blank book" and will fill it with your deepest desires, longings, introspections and prayers.

Chapter Two
Authentic Listening: Identifying *where* you are in life and where you want to be

"Apply your heart to instruction and your ears to words of knowledge."

Proverbs 23:12

Our roles alter over the years. To be fully alive, we must always be aware of the new directions we should go and fully embrace them. Furthermore, we must let go of those things that no longer serve us and serve those people with whom we are in relationship.

Tom Paterson, in *Living the Life You Were Meant to Live*, speaks of the seasons of our lives, describing them differently from what I had heard before. He designates winter as the time of early youth, "the years in which the soil of your life is prepared to receive information and to acquire skills." Spring is the time of education and preparation in schools, acquiring skills and information, similar to how valuable seeds are planted in a garden. Summer, he says, is the time of the work years, "the long, tedious, exhilarating, intense years of working at your craft and developing your giftedness." He concludes with the time of harvest—the later years. "These are the golden years of reaping from what you have sown. These are also the years of giving and sharing what you are reaping."[7]

No matter which season we find ourselves in, making the most of it involves looking carefully at who we are and how we can become our best selves.

"You have been shaped and fashioned for a specific mission," Paterson says, "but this mission changes from season to season in your life. Your giftedness does not change, but its *application* has phases."[8]

Being aware that change is coming involves learning to listen in multiple ways.

Learning to listen

When I was a child one of my favorite Bible stories was about the young boy Samuel hearing God's call during the night. Do you know the story? Samuel, who lived in the temple and assisted Eli the priest, was going to sleep when he heard someone call his name. He ran to Eli saying, "Here I am for you called me." Eli had not called Samuel and sent him back to bed. This happened again, and then on the third time, Eli realized Samuel was being called by God and told him:

"Go and lie down, and if he calls you, say, 'Speak, Lord, for your servant is listening.'" (Story in 1 Samuel 3:1-9)

Samuel did as he was told and the Lord revealed to him what was coming for Eli and his family. The account gives us two good examples to follow. Samuel listened to his mentor Eli and learned from him. Then Samuel listened to God and

---

[7] Tom Paterson, *Living the Life You Were Meant to Live* (Nashville: Thomas Nelson Publishers, 1998), 75.
[8] Ibid., 76.

obeyed, even though the message he had to deliver to Eli was an unhappy one.

As a child that story resonated with me—and it still does today. I want to hear and recognize the voice of God, and I want to be aware of those people around me who can lead me to understand how God wants to use me. Listening, then obeying God is essential if we are to become who we were created to be at all stages of life.

Listening as a life skill

One of the most underdeveloped skills in our arsenal of life tools is the ability to listen well. Most vocations and all relationships depend on good listening skills. For life coaches, therapists, counselors, teachers, preachers, parents—the list goes on and on—listening well is essential. And although it is such an important skill, few of us have actually had training in how to listen effectively.

We accuse our children (or our husbands) of selective hearing when we discover they've ignored our requests to clean their rooms or take out the garbage. But then we meet someone new and can't remember her name five minutes later. Did we hear it at all or were we too busy planning what we were going to say next, what we'll prepare for dinner—or whether those shoes go with that dress—to really listen?

Tony Stoltzfus, in *Leadership Coaching*, explains, "At first glance, listening may seem passive, but it is actually a powerful tool for solving problems. What often holds people back is not a lack of insight, but a lack of confidence in their own ideas or an inability to put them into words. The act of listening affirms and empowers people to express themselves with confidence."[9]

---

9   Tony Stoltzfus, *Leadership Coaching*, (available at www.Coach22.com, 2005), 147.

There are two important facets to listening. First we listen to others to affirm them and show respect, often helping them come to decisions in the process. Secondly we listen to gain information and direction for ourselves. So, whether we are listening to honor someone who is talking to us or listening to gain something for ourselves, learning to really hear at a deep level is a valuable skill.

According to the International Listening Association's website, (*Did you even know there is an International Listening Association?*), listening is "the process of receiving, constructing meaning from, and responding to spoken and/or nonverbal messages."[10]

I find it interesting that the idea of nonverbal messages is included in their definition of listening. We learn a lot from the body language of someone talking to us. In this case we're listening with our eyes, I suppose. To truly communicate, we need to use as many of our senses as possible. Even the sense of touch comes into play. A child will "hear" his mother through her loving embrace as much or more than through her words spoken into his ear.

By learning to actively listen, we can begin to minister to people who are seeking someone who cares and understands. We can become the body of Christ to those around us.

Tuning in, tuning out

The other side of listening, and the one we are most concerned with in this book, is listening to gain insight to who we are now and who we can become in the future.

We are bombarded daily with messages from the media as well as from people around us. We can't possibly absorb all

---

10   ILA, 1996. (www.listen.org).

that comes our way, so it's sometimes necessary to consciously decide what to listen to. Otherwise, if we're not careful, we may tune out at the wrong time and miss important information.

All our lives we have heard what others have said, even though we sometimes tried to ignore them. Hopefully, you've received positive, helpful messages along the way. But, maybe not. You may have been listening to the wrong people or hearing the wrong messages. Perhaps you are holding on to messages that were helpful as you were growing up but need to be discarded now. When you find yourself hesitating to do something because "Mom would not approve" or "Dad always said I'm not good enough to do that," you need to stop and evaluate those "parent messages." It's time to discard ideas that hold you back from being all you were created to be.

You may have suffered more serious abuse at the hands and mouths of those who should have nurtured, encouraged and protected you. If this is true, be assured that your past does not have to predict your future! You are free to choose who you will become. With God's healing—and with the help of a Christian therapist, if needed—you can overcome the things that would hold you back from being who God intended you to be.

Perhaps you don't receive put-downs from other people. Instead, *you* are the bearer of the negative messages. You tell yourself you couldn't possibly be successful at who you'd like to be. If it is a negative message about your value or your significance, you can know that it is not a message from the God who loves you unconditionally. Ask yourself where that message is coming from. Is it due to past failures in school? Did you begin believing the wrong messages during those difficult years in middle school, when you were searching for yourself? Be willing to dig deeply if necessary. Meaningful introspection takes time and quiet space, but it could make the difference between continuing to be held back by past limitations and soaring to new heights. Chapter Three of this book will address these issues in more depth.

Looking for a change and listening for a message

When you know it's time for a change in your life, how can you discover what direction you should go?

Sometimes we are overwhelmed with responsibilities and feel we have no energy or time to examine our lives. We may be caught in a job (or life) that doesn't fit, but we're afraid to change. We assume personality traits outside our true personality types, causing us to live less than authentic lives. We forget that there is a possibility of change. We've lost hope.

It's the American way. We work hard, move fast, don't slow down long enough to analyze whether or not what we're doing makes sense in the grand scheme of things, until something intrudes into our life, forcing us to stop. We talk more than we listen, sometimes asking questions and then not staying around long enough to hear the answers.

Even more detrimental in our lives is not hearing God's voice telling us who we are and what we can become. Occasionally, however, we may hear a whisper—a still small voice, perhaps. Somewhere, someone is inviting us to stop "doing" and just "be." If we don't take the time to listen for God's voice, we work in our own limited strength and fail to tap in to what God has prepared for us. We're sure we aren't smart enough or strong enough to do what we long to do—and we're right, we're not. But God has promised that we're not alone, that he has plans for us. Can we even begin to imagine the rich life God has in mind for each of us? Do we dare to believe what the writer of

Our life in ak. On the hives

1 Corinthians says: "No eye has seen, no ear has heard, no mind has conceived what God has prepared for those who love him" 1 Corinthians 2:9

Instead of traveling on autopilot all the time, do yourself the favor of taking some time to listen to your life. Are you where you want to be—where you thought you'd be at this stage? Where does the Creator God want you to be?

Spend some quality time to identify your feelings. Perhaps there are emotions you weren't allowed to express as a child or even as an adult. By listening to your past you can get clues of what you need to be in the present and the future. Let that knowledge guide you into a more fulfilling life. But in listening to the past, don't let it become a burden. Later we'll talk about making decisions and moving forward, but for now, just learn to listen.

The journey begins

So start the journey of discovery that can lead you out of your unsatisfying present life.

You may want to create a journal to record what you discover, as suggested in the questions section at the end of Chapter One. It doesn't need to be anything fancy. A spiral notebook with lines works for some women better than an Italian leather covered diary. You may even prefer to write on your computer and have a file called, "Journal" for your entries. Or how about recording your thoughts audibly in a digital recorder?

Don't worry about doing it every day if that intimidates you. This is a "No Guilt Zone." Write in a journal if you feel like it! Give yourself the freedom to write or not write. Draw pictures, if that helps. Some people are compulsive journal-ers (I wish I were), but others of us write sporadically. Confession time: I have about a dozen journals that have only the first few pages filled. I'm hopeless, I think, at true long-term journaling, but I've learned it can help immensely to put my thoughts on paper when I'm trying to make an important decision or just want clarification on an issue.

Learning to listen in a variety of ways

It's important for us to learn to listen to others to be able to support them, and it's also important for us to listen to outside sources to get support for ourselves. When we perceive a need for change in our lives, we start looking and listening for input that will help us know which direction to go.

"Most of the time we have a pretty clear idea what God is asking of us. *God initiates change* in our lives—He has a personalized change agenda for us and is always speaking and arranging circumstances to bring it to our attention,"[11] says Tony Stoltzfus, in *Leadership Coaching*.

In order to recognize where you are and where you want to go, you can tap into several different ways of listening—listening with your head, listening with your heart, listening to the wisdom of others, listening to scripture and listening to God through prayer and meditation, asking him to give you truth and direction in your life.

Listening to your head—What do you *think* you should be and do?

"You will keep in perfect peace him whose mind is steadfast, because he trusts in you." Isaiah 26:3

For some people, listening to their heads is easy. They operate best from the logical, left-brain. For others, it's more

---
11   Stoltzfus, 16.

difficult, but it's necessary for all of us. Although we don't want to listen *only* to our heads, we do need to hear from our logical side when analyzing where we are now and where we want to go. This is not your final decision-making, but only the beginning, exploring the possibilities.

It can be helpful to make a list of all the things you feel you should be and ask yourself why you feel this way. Keep asking 'why' until you get to your core values. Many Christians think their core values consist only of lofty ideals such as putting God and family first. While these things should certainly be true, it helps to go beyond these to the "second tier" things you enjoy in your life. Do you value beauty and/or creativity? When you are in the "great outdoors" do the cares of life slip away? Do you need animals around you?

For example, it could be something fairly simple. You might say, "I should volunteer to make cookies for my child's class at school. This is a worthwhile activity, but *why* do you think you should do this? If your answer has to do with feeling guilty because you turned down the teacher when she asked if you would help, that may not be good enough. If you're already coaching your child's soccer team, teaching his Sunday school class and directing the school play, it may be time for someone else to bake cookies. However, if your answer is, "I've been promising my child I would visit his class soon and I want to keep my promise," then it's time to fire up the oven.

Some of the items on your list may surprise you. If you take the time and space to think with an open mind, you will be able to get beyond the initial things that come easily, to those others that are hiding. There are no wrong answers. Write it all down. Do not allow the "I couldn't possibly really do this" thought to invade this sacred territory.

Let go of the "judge" telling you that you can't become *that person*. You're not smart enough, young enough, old enough, thin enough, wealthy enough… This is not the time to let the negatives draw you down. Just listen to the positive side of who you should be and what you should do with your life. There's time later to be practical if your ideas get outside the realm of reality.

List your abilities, talents and spiritual gifts. This will help you know what you would be good at doing.

If you're a choleric or melancholy type (see information about Personalities in Chapter One), this will be the way you most want to go about examining yourself. If you're a sanguine or phlegmatic, it might be more difficult, but still is meaningful.

Having an open mind and allowing that mind to guide you will lead to exciting discoveries as you get to know yourself better. Use a brainstorming approach in the beginning. Decide to be open to any ideas that come. Ideas can later be reined in if they're too far out there.

"Do not conform any longer to the pattern of this world, but be transformed by the renewing of your mind. Then you will be able to test and approve what God's will is—his good, pleasing and perfect will." Romans 12:2

Listening to your heart—What do you *wish* you could do?

"I pray also that the eyes of your heart may be enlightened in order that you may know the hope to which he has called you, the riches of his glorious inheritance in the saints," Ephesians 1:18

I love the image "the eyes of your heart." Do you take the time to "see" with your heart? This goes back to that idea of *passion* again. What do you feel strongly about? What keeps you awake at night (or would if you didn't crash every evening from sheer exhaustion)? What would you do if money were of no concern? Remember, you're just brainstorming now, so let all the dreams out of the cage where you've so carefully kept them. Did you have desires as a teenager that you've suppressed? Some of those dreams may have needed to die, but others may just need to be re-dreamed. Are there ideas lurking around the periphery of your consciousness that you haven't allowed to come forth? We'll look at this concept in greater depth in Chapter Six.

I was caught off-guard several years ago while looking through a group of prints in an art store. I was somewhat familiar with Brian Andreas' work of whimsical drawings and clever (sometimes outrageous) writings. When I got to one that said, "for a long time, she flew only when she thought no one else was watching," tears welled up and I quickly stifled an audible gasp. What was it about these words that caused such a reaction, I asked myself. It was an important question and I kept asking it until I had some resolution. I realized after lengthy introspection that I was not in the right job and had been afraid to face that fact. It was a good job—one that someone else would have loved having. But it was not the right place for me anymore. All my creative energy was stifled there, and I had not taken the time to use that creativity elsewhere. I have long believed that if I'm in the wrong place, whether as a volunteer or paid employee, that puts at least two people in the wrong place—me and the person who really should be in that position.

Because I listened to what my heart was telling me, I started searching for what I thought would be a better fit for my gifts and abilities. I subsequently left that position for a lower paying one on a church staff, but where my God-given talents were put to better use. In addition to the more administrative parts of my position as an assistant director of children's ministry, I helped paint murals, dramatized Biblical stories in costume and wrote Sunday school curriculum. I often found myself at the end of the workday with a smile on my face as I walked to my car. My heart was full of thanksgiving that God had provided such an avenue for the things I enjoyed so much.

After several years, I left that position to write and speak full time, but in the years on that church staff I received opportunities that prepared me for the move to writing and speaking. It had been the right place for the time, and I would have missed it if I had not listened to my heart.

Listening to others

Rather than going off in a direction that is unhealthy or simply wrong for you, test your idea with friends and family who truly have your best interest at heart. But be cautious. Sometimes friends and family mean well, but they discourage you from taking risks that might be necessary for you to reach your full potential.

When we were preparing to go to China to teach, even some Christian friends tried to talk us out of it. One lady at a church tea said to me in a rather haughty manner, "Why do you want to go all the way to China? There are plenty of people here in the U.S. who need to hear about Jesus." She was the wife of a retired minister and I was startled by her comment and attitude. I wanted to say, "But you're here to tell these people in the U.S.," but I smiled and kept silent. I've often wondered if she had once felt a tug towards international mission work and had refused it. What was in her past that caused her to seem so bitter about someone feeling called to go to China?

On the other hand, we had friends from the same church who encouraged us, prayed for us and wrote letters regularly while we were away. We were so blessed by their faithfulness in upholding us in what we felt called to do.

Friends and family members can be very helpful in discerning with you what God would have you do. Find those who will pray with you and hold you accountable to Biblical teachings and who truly have your best interests in mind.

Listening to scripture

When you feel God is leading in a certain direction, give it the litmus test. For the Christian, there's always the question: "Does it line up with scripture?" God will never ask you to do something that goes against his Word.

A friend of mine told me years ago of a married woman in her neighborhood who was considering having an affair with a married man. Both the woman and man were professing Christians.

"God has provided him for me because I'm so unhappy in my marriage," the woman declared to my friend.

But God doesn't work that way, and my friend told her so. Just thinking of how many people would have been hurt by that affair can give a mature Christian pause. But it's easy to let irrationality intrude when our emotions are overloaded. We hear only what we want to hear sometimes, rationalizing by saying, *"If God loves me, He wants me to be happy."*

God does want us to be happy, I believe. That's why he gave us the Biblical concepts of how we should live. For that reason, it's good to be grounded in God's word *before* facing temptation. It's also important, of course, not to pull verses out of context, but to let the scriptures speak *to* us, not be manipulated *by* us.

Psalms 139:5 is one of my favorite verses: "You hem me in—behind and before; you have laid your hand upon me." While some people might interpret this verse as confining, to me it is a reminder that God protects me and guides me as I go through life.

The year we lived in China, we would occasionally go downtown to shop. We didn't do it very often because it was a bit of a struggle. In the town where we lived there were very few foreigners, so we caused quite a stir. The area was always crowded with pedestrians and bicyclists vying for space. We often compared it to trying to get through the throng at a rock concert or other packed event. And since we were obviously not Chinese and many of the citizens of that city had never seen foreigners, we were objects of intense interest—especially our children. We learned that the easiest way to move through the crowd was to walk single file, with my husband, Daryl, going in front and holding his arms down and back. I went last, reaching forward and grasping his hands, making a "cage" for the children to walk in. This kept the children safe from friendly but curious people who wanted to touch them, and it also kept us all together, lest the children get lost among the hundreds of people on the sidewalks.

"You hem me in…" What comforting words.

A companion verse to that, in my mind, is Psalm 119:32—"I run in the path of your commands, for you have set my heart free." Once we know what God has commanded us in the scriptures, we are free to run down the path he has given us. God never intended for us to live small lives, but instead calls us to dream big dreams and carry out his purposes for our lives.

Many times as I read my Bible certain phrases will "jump off the page" and seem as if they were written just for me. When that happens, I write them down in my journal or on the flyleaf of my Bible, so I can re-visit those thoughts. Those verses are good ones to meditate on from time to time as I ask God to guide me and give me new insight for my life.

By listening to scripture, I can learn more of how God wants to use me for his service.

Listening to your Father

In her book, *When the Soul Listens*, Jan Johnson reminds us that God is always with us, just waiting for us to recognize that fact.

Only because we are unable to see God with our fallen eyes do we invent the idea of 'visiting' God now and then at church, retreats, and official moments of prayer. When we talk about 'entering God's presence,' we speak as if there are places where God is not…The problem is not that God goes away, but that we are unaware of His presence.[12]

While you're taking the time to contemplate where you are in life, as mentioned earlier, ask God to guide you and speak to your heart. If this is a new discipline for you, don't worry about saying the right words or having the right posture, just speak to God as you would to a friend in the same room with you. Sit in a favorite chair or outside on the grass, or wherever you feel comfortable. Anywhere you decide to stop and reflect, God is already there and is eager to hear from you.

---

12   Jan Johnson, *When the Soul Listens* (Colorado Springs, CO.: NavPress, 1999) 73-74.

Listening for the voice of God is the most important thing we can do in becoming authentic—the persons we were created to be. Yet, we let other things get in the way of this essential communication. Too often we wait until a crisis arises before we turn to God and ask for help. And even then, we may be more interested in telling God what he needs to do rather than listening to God's leading. You and I might even get sidetracked along the way and forget to show up for our prayer time, but God does not. No matter where we are, God is already there. We need to know—"If I rise on the wings of the dawn, if I settle on the far side of the sea, even there your hand will guide me, your right hand will hold me fast." Psalm 139:9-10

This verse became very important to me when we were preparing to teach in China. We struggled for many months, trying to discern if it was indeed God's will for us at the time. I had felt a heart-tug suggesting that and tried to dismiss it again and again, but the feeling kept coming back. We needed to know that it was truly God speaking to us, saying 'Go' and also that wherever we went, God would go before us.

It was amazing how many different ways we had the idea reinforced—songs on the radio, sermons, friends' comments, magazine articles... Yes, of course, we were tuned in to that subject, but I think God used many different circumstances to assure us of his love and faithfulness.

During that time we saw in a magazine a quotation attributed to John A. Shedd that said, "Ships in the harbor are safe, but that's not what ships are built for." Because of this and all the other things we had seen and heard, we felt that God was telling us, "Don't worry about safety, instead be concerned about following my will."

We spent a very rewarding year teaching in the People's Republic of China, followed by years and years of great memories, because we listened to the voice of our loving Father.

Sometimes we're afraid to pray because we're afraid God will call us to do something we don't want to do. We're afraid of the change that might be on the horizon. In *Hearing God: Developing a Conversational Relationship with God*, Dallas Willard says, "If we do not want to be converted from our chosen and habitual ways, if we really want to run our own lives without any interference from God, our very perceptual mechanisms will filter out his voice or twist it to our own purposes."[13]

Or we may feel we can't pray because our prayers are trivial and we don't want to bother God with them. Willard continues, saying, "Nothing is too insignificant or too hopeless to bring before God. Share all things with God by lifting them to him in prayer, and ask for his guidance even—or perhaps especially—in those things that you think you already understand."[14]

So if you're eager to know what to do with your life—how to become the person you were created to be—pray, pray and pray some more. And as you pray, don't do all the talking. Spend time with the Father in silence and let him speak to you.

Sometimes his answer is No

Listening and obeying

Because of our year in China, we have an ongoing interest in the Chinese language, in spite of the difficulty of speaking, reading and writing. My ability is extremely limited, but I sometimes find a word that "speaks" to me in a special way. While doing research for this book I came across the website for the

---

13   Dallas Willard, *Hearing God: Developing a Conversational Relationship with God* (Downers Grove, IL: InterVarsity Press, 1999), 197.
14   Ibid., 214.

International Listening Association, mentioned earlier. I was intrigued by the Chinese character on their website for "listen"—pronounced "ting" in Mandarin Chinese.

This Chinese character for "listen" (聽) contains a combination of the characters (words) for "ear" and "heart." (And even the character for "eye" is turned on its side and included.) What a beautiful representation of what it is to truly listen to someone.

Furthermore, this same character can mean "obey." I have posted this Chinese word over my computer to remind me to "listen and obey" when I hear God speak to me. What good is it to hear the voice of God if we're not willing to obey his commands? (No, I don't hear an audible voice, but I sometimes have a deep impression of a spiritual word from God. Mentally, I talk back—usually saying something highly spiritual like, "You gotta be kidding! You can't really mean I should do that!" or "Is this really you, God, or am I making this up?")

This close alliance between listening and obeying was reinforced when I happened upon the etymology of the word "obey." According to The American Heritage Dictionary of the English Language, the word "obey" comes from words meaning "to listen to."[15] As a parent I used to ask my children, "Do you hear me?" when I often meant "You'd better obey me, if you know what's good for you." I think God does a similar thing. He wants us to listen and obey, because he knows what's best. God has great blessings in store for us when we are willing to accept them.

Like young Samuel in the temple, we must learn to recognize the voice of God, then obey his word to us even if that

---

15 *The American Heritage Dictionary of the English Language*, Fourth Edition. (Houghton Mifflin Company).

means stepping outside of our comfort zone. By trusting that God loves us and wants to do good things for us and through us, we step out in faith to do what we are called to do.

In the next chapter, "Authentic Bearing: Standing tall with confidence," we will see several contemporary women who listened carefully and made changes in their lives, discovering in the process that God's plans for them were better than they could have imagined.

ACTION STEPS:
Questions to help you listen—

Give yourself some quiet time to think about these questions. Consider writing in your journal about what you learn.

1. What season of life are you in right now, according to Tom Patterson's descriptions near the beginning of this chapter?
2. In what areas of your life do you need to listen carefully?
3. What are some messages you've heard over the years that have not been helpful in your personal growth?
4. What put-downs do you hear coming from yourself and with what will you replace these negative messages?
5. Do you find it easier to listen to your head or your heart?
6. What do your friends and family say you should do or be? Have you seriously considered doing it? Does it align with your deep, heartfelt desires?

Chapter Three
Authentic Bearing: Standing tall with confidence—going beyond self-esteem to God's esteem

"What good would it do to get everything you want and lose you, the real you?"
Luke 9:25 (THE MESSAGE)

> *At fifteen she began her modeling career.*
> *At sixteen she was living in Paris, gracing the covers of top fashion magazines.*
> *At eighteen she was planning how she would commit suicide.*

Tonya Ruiz received her first Barbie doll at age three and it quickly became her favorite toy. Many Barbies followed that first one, including one that said, "I love being a fashion model." During her early teen years, Tonya thought if she could be as beautiful as Barbie, life would be perfect.

She was fifteen when she started modeling classes, and she soon was modeling in Paris, Munich, Tokyo, Beverly Hills and New York. With her image on the cover of magazines and

THE AUTHENTIC YOU: Becoming the Woman You Were Created to Be

billboards, her nights were filled with parties, dancing alongside rock stars and royalty. Tonya had gained success—at least success as many would define it.

However, there was a dark side.

"Soon after I'd arrived in Paris, I felt something was missing from my life. No matter where I lived, whom I dated, or what success I achieved, I felt empty. I used food to fill that empty place, and eventually I turned to alcohol, drugs, and men. My life spiraled downward."[16]

Modeling lessons had not prepared her for standing tall with confidence.

After seeking fulfillment in ways that only brought further emptiness, Tonya decided her best option was suicide. She left Europe, returning to Southern California to say goodbye to her family, but her life was saved because a friend cared enough to invite her to attend a concert at a local church.

In the gospel message given after the concert, Tonya learned that God loved her and could redeem her life. The pastor quoted John 3:16, "For God so loved the world that he gave his one and only Son, that whoever believes in him shall not perish but have eternal life."

"I had grown up going to church," Tonya says, "and I knew all the hymns, but I did not ever remember hearing about how to be born again. If it was mentioned, I was not listening. Never had I heard the truth explained so simply."[17]

That night, accompanied by her friend, she walked to the front of the room and confessed her sins, opening her life to Christ.

---

16 Tonya Ruiz, *Today's Christian Woman*, "Beyond Barbie," (November/December, Vol. 27, No. 6, 2005), 70.

17 Tonya Ruiz, *A Model's Journey* (Garden Grove, CA: Zephaniah Company, 2001), 122.

Tonya's life took a 180 degree turn. Instead of being obsessed about her weight or her looks, as she had been for several years, she began to see herself through God's eyes. Seeking God's will for her life eventually led to a path she would never have dreamed of earlier—becoming a pastor's wife.

Now Tonya is passionate about using her experiences to help others. As a self-proclaimed "Barbiologist," she speaks to women of all ages about the danger of believing the hype about what the ideal woman should look like. Using humor and candor, she tells her story and encourages women to recognize their true beauty as God's magnificent one-of-a-kind creations. God is using her and her experiences to influence women who are caught in the lies that come with comparing ourselves to others.

Comparing ourselves to others

Why do we continually compare ourselves to others? From an early age we are taught the importance of evaluating things. *Is this head of lettuce better than that one? Does that school prepare me for my career better than this one? Will that man treat me in the future the way he treats his mother now?*

It makes sense to compare some things, but when we compare ourselves to those around us we run into trouble. We build ourselves up in our own minds by looking at someone who appears to be on a lower rung of the ladder, then we condemn ourselves as being unworthy when we look at the people we've placed on higher rungs. Either way we take our focus off of the God who loves us and who has great plans in mind for us, using our unique capabilities.

Making peace with who we are now

"Tell us how to make peace with the faces we see in the mirror at this age in our lives," a friend said to me as we talked about this book.

It is part of that same question we've asked since we were teenagers. How do I look: better or worse than the other girls in the room? However, we are not just comparing ourselves with others our age, we're looking at models and Hollywood starlets on magazine covers who may be half our age or less and whose air-brushed photographs are not even reality!

Do you remember the movie, *Death Becomes Her*, starring Goldie Hawn and Meryl Streep? This spoof about preserving youth and beauty at any cost is our generation's answer to Oscar Wilde's Dorian Gray character. When we become consumed by our outward appearance at the expense of inner growth, we become hollow caricatures of our true selves—of what we can be.

We're looking to the wrong role models and holding up impossible goals. It's time for us to make peace with the inner and outer selves God created us to be at every age. If not, we will miss the amazing opportunities we have in front of us—growing spiritually, developing a deeper relationship with God, mentoring others—because we are looking backward and trying to hold on to what we had in the past.

Yes, I think it's good for us to look our best, as a reflection of who we are—God's workmanship. But when outer beauty comes at the expense of knowing who we are in Christ, it has taken on a life bigger than God intended.

Tonya Ruiz reminds us, "The world's definition of physical beauty changes with the seasons. God's definition of spiritual beauty is unchanged and eternal—He has different criteria for measuring beauty. High-chiseled cheekbones do not make you a better person. Wearing the latest fashions will not benefit you spiritually. God is concerned about you being included on a list of 'Beautiful People'—SPIRITUALLY 'Beautiful People' with hearts who seek after him...Women who love the Lord have a beauty and glow about them that cannot be purchased at the cosmetic counter."[18]

Trying to please others

When we don't have a sense of our own worth we look outward for others to tell us who we are.

"What is the result of failing to reject society's standards and adopt godly standards?" asks author Sharon Fawcett. "For me, it was more than three decades of dysfunction, three years with an eating disorder, and nine years with depression and an obsessive compulsive personality disorder."[19]

Sharon shares her remarkable story in her book, *Hope for Wholeness: The Spiritual Path to Freedom from Depression.* She says she overcame her battle with anorexia nervosa by learning that her "worth was not found in her appearance but as a beautiful child of the King."[20]

In spite of living an active life with a loving husband and two adorable young daughters, Sharon slipped into an abyss—clinical depression. Her daughters were one and four years old when she was first hospitalized for depression. Over the next nine years she would fight to emerge from the state she describes as "an empty arrangement of bones dressed in skin—warm, breathing, and moveable but devoid of any spark of life."[21]

---

18   Ibid., 189.

19   Sharon Fawcett, personal correspondence with the author.

20   Ibid.

21   Sharon Fawcett, *Hope for Wholeness: The Spiritual Path to Freedom from Depression* (Colorado Springs, CO: NavPress, 2008), 22.

Through extensive counseling and therapy, Sharon came out of the nightmare of depression and now speaks and writes to help other women dealing with this illness. In her book she says, "Looking back, from the other side of depression, I'm able to better understand how the pieces of my personality fit together to make me a perfect candidate for the illness. One of the roots of my depression was a low sense of self-worth, which affected almost every aspect of my being, behavior, and relationships."[22]

Sharon encourages women to examine their lives and get help early if they feel depressed for more than a short period of time. She warns that too often we try to take care of matters by ourselves without seeking others for help. Christians may feel they can't admit they are depressed, especially in their churches, as that would show weakness and lack of a proper spiritual life.

Sharon says, "Whether biochemistry, emotional wounds, or spiritual matters have caused your depression, be assured that it is not a punishment. God doesn't want you to suffer from this illness or any other. Even though experiencing brokenness, sickness, and despair is part of the reality of living in a fallen world, God can use these times to change us for the better. Don't underestimate His ability or His plans for you."[23]

Reaching for perfection

Too many of us seek physical perfection—a goal that is impossible to attain. When we can't have perfect bodies, perfect careers, perfect houses, perfect gardens, perfect relationships, perfect children, we look to other false ways of filling our longings.

---

22   Ibid., 103.
23   Ibid., 39.

We may use food, shopping, drugs, unhealthy relationships or other means in hopes of feeling fulfilled.

In *Fresh-Brewed Life: A Stirring Invitation to Wake Up Your Soul*, Nicole Johnson helps us see how we can learn from our own lives by observing our longings. "When I eat too much or buy too much or obsess about the way I look, I am trying to fill up my longing for wholeness. I want to have all I need and more. I don't want to feel empty or lacking or less than perfect."[24]

The inner self

For most of us, our inner selves are not consistent with our outer selves. We may appear strong and secure to others while inside we feel inadequate. Even within ourselves there is sometimes a war going on.

According to psychologist Dr. Gerald May, "Many of us feel a tremendous ambivalence about this inner self. On the one hand, we are sometimes convinced both psychologically and spiritually that the true self is basically good, that it means well, and that it is capable of considerable creativity and beauty. On the other hand, our daily emotional sense is often that 'who I really am' is not quite up to par. It is somehow defective, not quite as worthwhile as it could or should be. This vague sense of defectiveness results in some degree of compensation, some effort at making ourselves presentable and acceptable to others."[25]

Facing the fears

Outward appearance is not the only area where we beat ourselves up, unfortunately. In a recent workshop I conducted,

---

24   Nicole Johnson, *Fresh-Brewed Life: A Stirring Invitation to Wake Up Your Soul* (Nashville, Tennessee: Thomas Nelson, Inc., 1999, 55.
25   Gerald May, MD, *Will and Spirit* (HarperSanFrancisco, 1982), 73.

I asked women to complete this sentence. "I can't follow my dream because _____."

The answers were typical of what I had seen in previous workshops. *I'm not smart enough. I'm too old. I don't have enough education. I'm afraid of what someone might think of me. I'd probably fail. I'm afraid I'll succeed and won't be able to handle the consequences.*

We limit ourselves by our fears of not being good enough, and as a result of negative self-talk we hold ourselves back from being all we were created to be. What if we talked to our friends the way we talk to ourselves?

"You're not smart enough."

"You're too old."

"You'd probably fail."

Not many friendships would survive that kind of abuse. Yet we talk to ourselves regularly like this.

We read in the Bible that we should love our neighbors as ourselves. I wonder if our neighbors would want to be treated the way we treat ourselves?

Think about it—if we don't truly love ourselves appropriately, maybe we had better not try to love our neighbors as ourselves. Our neighbors want better treatment!

Self-esteem vs. God's esteem

The subject of self-esteem has gotten a bad rap lately in some Christian circles, but how you feel about yourself plays a large part in how you meet your world.

Too many women have little sense of self-worth because they don't understand or can't accept the depth of God's love for them. They are still carrying around toxic opinions of themselves held over from earlier experiences and of society's ideas of what a beautiful, successful woman should look like, act like and be like. They are listening to others' opinions and believing what they hear.

The Middle School muddle and beyond
Middle School can be brutal. At this crucial time when teens are developing who they are, they are extremely vulnerable and are often cruel to one another. They look around to see how they fit into the hierarchy of popularity and no matter where they are in the pecking order, they rarely feel secure.

What was it like for you during those grades? Did you fear being made fun of by other girls in your gym class? Were you the one chosen first or last for teams? For me, even the fear at the beginning of the year of forgetting my locker number or where my classes were located or what order they were in caused enough panic to result in recurring dreams for years.

Some of us are still hearing those old messages from parents, teachers and others, telling us that we aren't good enough, smart enough, thin enough, talented enough, fast enough, strong enough. On and on it goes. If that's true for you, it's time to leave those negative messages behind and get new input.

Our brains, it seems, use the path of least resistance when a thought comes our way. For instance, if I've always thought along a path that says, *I made a mistake; that proves I'm really stupid*, the next time I make a mistake, that's the most likely path my mind will take. But I can re-program my brain. With purposeful re-thinking, I can train my brain to understand the truth, *I made a mistake; everyone makes mistakes. This is just one incident. It does not determine my overall ability.* I won't change long-held habits overnight, but with repeated reinforcement of this new way of thinking, I can overcome my negative response.

As I talk with women in Bible studies, after speaking engagements and in life coaching sessions, my heart grieves because of what many have experienced.

Recently, at a luncheon for Christian speakers and writers, an elegant and very stylish woman in her eighties confessed to those of us at the table that she had only lately begun to express her true self. She had been ridiculed by her mother and sister all her life and had never been able to meet their expectations. But now that they had both died, she was moving forward with long strides, planning to write books. We applauded her new-found freedom and her courage to do what she felt led to do. How sad, though, that she had waited this long before being able to come forth and be her authentic self.

In contrast, another woman I met not long ago is still suffering from the emotional abuse she has received from family members throughout her life. She believed the lies she was told as she was growing up, that she was stupid and not worth anything, and she still holds a low opinion of herself. It may be *her* opinion, it may be *her family's* opinion, but *it is not God's opinion* about who she is and how worthy she is.

Through coaching I have worked with women in their twenties and thirties, or beyond, who are dealing with similar issues. Hopefully, each woman will be able to move from the mindset of not being "enough" to knowing that she is a talented, capable person with the ability to do extraordinary things. This takes intentional work to reset the value meter each of us carries within.

Parents, siblings or teachers may have said hurtful things to you. However, there are times when we interpret statements negatively even though they were not intended that way. Whether intended as putdowns or not, we can re-frame or re-interpret those events that have caused us pain. To do this it is necessary to think back to the event and claim a different take-away for ourselves. For instance, the person making negative comments is often working out of fear, pain or even jealousy. By recognizing that, and with God's help, we can let go of our own pain and move on to a healthy sense of self-worth.

Often it is more effective to have a friend, coach or therapist to help us work through these issues, so don't hesitate to ask for help. If you have experienced negative situations that tend to cripple you, there's hope. You can become the person you were created to be. You no longer have to believe the lies others have said about you—or the things that you interpreted as put-downs.

Your future does not have to depend upon what others thought about you in your past or even what they think of you today. You can determine to replace others' opinion of you with God's opinion.

We need to know, believe and understand that God loves us. God *is* love. When we grasp this truth, a whole new world opens to us.

So if you feel you have been robbed of self-esteem, replace it with an understanding of what God thinks of you—God's esteem.

Created in God's Image

In her book, *Knowing God: Making God the Main Thing in My Life,* Kimberly Dunnam Reisman says, "The entire biblical witness is to the reality of God staying with us, through God's grace pursuing us, loving us, desiring to restore us to the selves we were created to be, to bring us back into relationship with God."[26]

If you do not believe that you are created in the image of God and that he has a wonderful plan for your life, immerse yourself in his letter to you—the Bible—and absorb what God thinks of you until you can believe it for yourself.

Regal bearing—

Do we fearlessly claim our places as daughters of the king, created in the very image of God? Or instead, do we feel we have to earn the right to be part of God's family? Do we step boldly into our calling, standing tall, or do we sit in the cinders, allowing others to tell us who we are, waiting for a fairy-godmother to change us so that we are acceptable to the other members of the kingdom?

Becoming authentic Christian women means we accept that God created us for his purposes. Understanding ourselves is indispensable if we are to become who God created us to be, so continue the journey with me.

In the next chapter we'll see how giving and receiving forgiveness is an integral part of becoming all we were created to be.

ACTION STEPS:

Questions to Help You Move from Self-Esteem to God's Esteem

To begin understanding God's Esteem, take some quiet time to think about and answer the following questions. You may want to add this to the journal entries you started in the earlier chapters of this book.

---

26   Kimberly Dunnam Reisman, *Knowing God: Making God the Main Thing in My Life* (Nashville, TN: Abingdon Press, 2003), 40.

Authentic Bearing: Standing tall with confidence

1. How do you feel about yourself right now?
2. Do you frequently replay old messages that tell you negative things about yourself? What do they sound like?
3. Are you holding back from living fully because of fear, insecurity or thinking that you don't deserve success?
4. If you haven't done so already, make a list of your gifts, talents and abilities. Get a friend to help if you have trouble recognizing your own abilities.
5. Thank God for your uniqueness and ask how you can best use your gifts.
6. Make a list of your big and small successes from the last two weeks. (If you're feeling down, a success might be just getting dressed each morning.)
7. Read and meditate on scriptures that tell how God loves you and wants to use you in significant ways. (See sidebar for some verses.)

> **Look at what the Bible says about us—**
>
> "So God created man in his own image, in the image of God he created him; male and female he created them... God saw all that he had made, and it was very good." Genesis 1:27, 31a
>
> "When God created man, he made him in the likeness of God. He created them male and female and blessed them. And when they were created he called them 'man.'" Genesis 5:1-2
>
> "For you created my inmost being; you knit me together in my mother's womb. I praise you because I am fearfully and wonderfully made; your works are

8. Create reminder cards listing encouraging scriptures and put them on your mirror, computer, car dashboard, or other places to remind you that you are a valuable member of God's kingdom.
9. Look for ways to use your abilities to help others.
10. Thank God at least three times a day for life, air, beauty and other blessings in your life.

wonderful, I know that full well." Psalm 139:13-14

"But because of his great love for us, God, who is rich in mercy, made us alive with Christ even when we were dead in transgressions—it is by grace you have been saved." Ephesians 2:4-5

"Therefore, if anyone is in Christ, he is a new creation; the old has gone, the new has come!" 2 Corinthians 5:17

"For we are God's workmanship, created in Christ Jesus to do good works, which God prepared in advance for us to do." Ephesians 2:10

"Therefore, there is now no condemnation for those who are in Christ Jesus, because through Christ Jesus the law of the Spirit of life set me free from the law of sin and death." Romans 8:1-2

"Do you not know that your body is a temple of the Holy Spirit, who is in you, whom you have received from God? You are not your own; you were bought at a price. Therefore honor God with your body." 1 Corinthians 6:19-20

Chapter Four
Authentic Forgiving: Offering Forgiveness and Grace—Accepting Forgiveness and Grace

"Then Peter came to Jesus and asked, 'Lord, how many times shall I forgive my brother when he sins against me? Up to seven times?' Jesus answered, 'I tell you, not seven times but seventy-seven times.'"

Matthew 18:21-22

Unforgiveness reveals itself in the set jaw, the narrowed eyes, the cold shoulder, the slammed door, the premature divorce. It crawls in and makes its lair within us. It lurks in the dark corners of our memories. And we refuse to release it. Instead we feed it, finger its mane, sharpen its claws. Then, when we least expect it, without our permission or knowledge, it begins to feed on us, slowly devouring us as it grows stronger and stronger.[27]

Steven James
Becoming Real: Christ's Call to Authentic Living

---

[27] Steven James, *Becoming Real: Christ's Call to Authentic Living* (Monroe, Louisiana: Howard Publishing Company, Inc., 2005), 147.

If we are going to live authentic lives, to be the women God created us to be, we will have to learn to forgive and be forgiven, enabling us to move beyond events that stunt our emotional and spiritual growth.

Learning to forgive others

Forgiveness. It's a word commonly used but often misunderstood. We have trouble differentiating between condoning behaviors and forgiving—letting go of the bitterness that keeps us from moving forward in our lives. Often we want to hold on to our resentments and anger. We can even harbor thoughts of vengeance and hatred.

When I read the book, *The Hiding Place*, I was struck by a model of forgiveness from the life of Corrie ten Boom. The ten Boom family had sheltered Jews in their small home in the Netherlands during World War II. Arrested and sent eventually to Ravensbruck Concentration Camp, Corrie survived, but her sister Betsie died there.

During the postwar period, as Corrie worked for reconciliation in Europe, she spoke in many places, telling the story of Betsie's desire to help people after the war and of how healing came with forgiveness. Then in Munich at a church service, she came face to face with one of the former German guards from Ravensbruck.

> He came up to me as the church was emptying, beaming and bowing. "How grateful I am for your message, *Fraulein.*" He said. "To think that, as you say, He has washed my sins away!"
>
> His hand was thrust out to shake mine. And I, who had preached so often to the people in Bloemendaal the need to forgive, kept my hand at my side.

Authentic Forgiving: Offering Forgiveness and Grace

> ...
>
> I tried to smile, I struggled to raise my hand. I could not. I felt nothing, not the slightest spark of warmth or charity. And so again I breathed a silent prayer. *Jesus, I cannot forgive him. Give Your forgiveness.*
>
> As I took his hand the most incredible thing happened. From my shoulder along my arm and through my hand, a current seemed to pass from me to him, while into my heart sprang a love for this stranger that almost overwhelmed me.[28]

What a demonstration of how God can use us as vessels of his love when we're willing to forgive.

The apostle Paul understood the toxic nature of an unforgiving spirit and exhorted the Ephesians to "Get rid of all bitterness, rage and anger, brawling and slander, along with every form of malice. Be kind and compassionate to one another, forgiving each other, just as in Christ God forgave you." Ephesians 4:31-32

Counselor, writer and speaker Jami Kirkbride recounts her realization that forgiveness can come differently from how we expect it. When told of her ex-husband's death she was faced with a myriad of emotions. The memories of abuse she and her son had suffered at his hands, until her divorce seven years before, was mixed with concern for her ex-husband's present family.

At one time she had thought she would be able to forgive him if he admitted what he had done and asked for forgiveness, but that never happened. One week before his death he called

---

28   Corrie ten Boom, *The Hiding Place* (Grand Rapids, MI: Chosen Books, Fourth Printing, March 2008), 247-248.

Jami. It was a call that helped her realize that she didn't even need for him to ask for forgiveness.

> I always thought the path to forgiveness would be as I imagined, with the right admissions getting the right responses. But God, in His grace, had a whole different plan. The phone call made me realize how God lovingly and gently brought my heart to a place of forgiveness. It was not dependent on anything my ex-husband did. It wasn't even important for him to ask for my forgiveness. Those things didn't matter any more. I knew then, it was not of my own power. I had not conjured up some spiritual strength to grant forgiveness. God had slowly and steadily transformed my heart with His grace. The same grace He extends to forgive each of us.[29]

We are often told that love is not a feeling; it's a choice. We can choose to love someone who seems unlovable, and in the same way, we can choose to forgive someone who has hurt us, whether or not they ever acknowledge the pain they caused. We forgive others for our own good—to empty our hearts of the poison residing there. With God's help, we release the crippling hate that keeps us from becoming whole. Pouring all the anger and frustration onto the pages of your journal may help you begin the healing process that will allow you to move beyond the pain. The questions at the end of this chapter can help guide you to a place of release and restoration.

---

[29] *When God Steps In: True Stories of Transformation by God's Grace*, compiled by Linda Gilden (Belleville, Ontario, Canada: Essence Publishing, 2006), 45.

Accepting forgiveness from others

"Hello, my name is Nancy, and I am a cheater. I've never cheated on a tax return or a final exam, but I did cheat on my husband. That's why I'm an expert on infidelity—because I've lived it."[30]

Thus begins Nancy C. Anderson's book, *Avoiding the Greener Grass Syndrome*.

While having an affair with a male friend from her workplace, Nancy was confronted by her parents about her decision to leave her husband. Having grown up in a Christian home, Nancy knew she was not living the way she had been taught. Eventually, she realized she was tired of lying and prayed for God to show her the way out of her sin and to restore her marriage.

Nancy has written her book to help couples understand how easily infidelity can happen and how they can prevent it. She admits that she didn't work on her marriage before she got to the place where she almost lost it. A second message of the book is that there is hope after infidelity. Nancy confessed to her husband and asked him to forgive her, which he did. Even so, they had to work hard at reconciliation and re-wiring their communication in order to create a good marriage.

"Since our reconciliation in 1980," Nancy says, "we've completely rebuilt our marriage. We had to destroy the old foundation—selfishness—and rebuild upon the rock—Jesus. We used a perfect blueprint—the Bible—and now our home stands firm."[31]

---

30 Nancy C. Anderson, *Avoiding the Greener Grass Syndrome* (Grand Rapids, MI: Kregel Publications, 2004), 13.
31 Ibid., 46.

Accepting God's forgiveness

For some women, it is easier to forgive others than to accept forgiveness—especially the very real forgiveness that comes from our Creator. God's saving grace is the initial forgiveness we must receive in order for the other elements of forgiveness to work properly. The Bible is full of stories of people who sought and received God's forgiveness.

People who are not familiar with the Bible often have misconceptions about its contents. Some think it is a book full of stories about how God is "out to get us." Others think it is a book about the lives of saints who have done no wrong. Both of these views are far from the truth. Biblical people are just like us, in relationship with the same God—the one who wants to draw us near and who continually reaches out to us in our stress-filled, busy lives with an invitation to be forgiven and experience peace in spite of what we've done.

The Old Testament hero David was known as a man after God's own heart, yet he was guilty of coveting another man's wife; adultery with that woman, Bathsheba; and murdering her husband, Uriah. All three of these sins went against the foundational commandments given to Moses by God for the Israelites. David, King of Israel, chose to break those laws.

When we read about David, we see that at first he tried to hide his sins, but when confronted about it he understood the depth of his wrong-doing. In deep agony, David recognized his own sin and realized how far he had fallen from God's ideal. He then repented and begged God for forgiveness and renewal.

Cecil Murphey in *The God Who Pursues* says, "We can also learn from the situation with David that when the

Authentic Forgiving: Offering Forgiveness and Grace

Holy confronts us, the pain may be so great that it may seem as if there is no forgiveness. It appears that the morning will never break again, and that it will always be midnight."[32]

But we learn from David's story that morning does come.

When we sin—and we will—we can pray with David, "Have mercy on me, O God, according to your unfailing love; according to your great compassion blot out my transgressions. Wash away all my iniquity and cleanse me from my sin. For I know my transgressions, and my sin is always before me. Against you, you only, have I sinned and done what is evil in your sight, so that you are proved right when you speak and justified when you judge...Hide your face from my sins and blot out all my iniquity. Create in me a pure heart, O God, and renew a steadfast spirit within me. Do not cast me from your presence or take your Holy Spirit from me. Restore to me the joy of your salvation and grant me a willing spirit, to sustain me." Psalm 51:1-4, 9-12

Notice that David prayed not only for renewal but for a willing spirit. When we understand that we have sinned and that all sin is really against God, we can claim God's promises of renewal and ask God to help us in the future to follow the right path before us.

If David, in spite of his failings, was a man after God's own heart, is there a chance that we are women after God's own heart as well? Since God forgave David and used him in a mighty way, can we see that God can use us, too, no matter what we've done in the past?

---

[32] Cecil Murphey, *The God Who Pursues* (Bloomington, Minnesota: Bethany House Publishers), 157.

Complete forgiveness

"I, even I, am he who blots out your transgressions, for my own sake, and remembers your sins no more." Isaiah 43:25

Can we accept God's forgiveness *and forgive ourselves* so we can move on in a positive direction and truly become the persons God has created us to be—our authentic selves? God offers complete forgiveness when we repent. Our sins—all our sins—are forgiven.

Measuring sin

Hate, gossip, abortion, lying, adultery, cheating—we usually think of some sins as being greater than others. We may feel that God overlooks the "little" sins. But all sin separates us from God. If we want to be all we can be, we must repent of all sin and ask God to give us strength in overcoming our tendencies to live apart from God's plan.

And then there are those "hidden sins." There are things we have kept secret from everyone but God. Hidden sins are destructive. They will keep us from spiritual growth and from fellowship with God. We need to take inventory from time to time, do a heart-search, to see if we are harboring resentments, hatred, jealousy, covetousness or other silent sins. When these and other shortcomings show up on our lists, we can come before the loving Father, repent and have fellowship restored.

Another misconception about sin is that God can forgive the so-called little sins but not the big ones. King David's story tells us otherwise. We usually (and incorrectly) consider murder a sin bigger than others, but God forgave David of this and all the other sins he committed. He will do the same for us when we turn from our sin and ask for forgiveness.

Authentic Forgiving: Offering Forgiveness and Grace

God's gracious gift vs. earning God's love

We sometimes try to earn God's love and forgiveness by doing things "for God." We work and work and still don't feel like we deserve God's love. We're right! We don't deserve God's love. Fortunately, that's not the plan God put in place.

God's forgiveness is a gift, not something we can earn. The idea that we must do enough good to outweigh the bad we've done is not a biblical concept. Yet, we hear that over and over in the popular culture. It even seeps into our churches. We may agree to do too many activities and head too many committees, hoping God will accept us or love us more.

You do play a part—not by doing enough good to make up for your sins, but by making a conscious choice to turn away from those sins and accept the grace God offers. God extends this grace to you no matter what your past looks like, through the life, death, and resurrection of Jesus, the Christ. Your part is to decide you want to accept that grace and exchange your old life for a new one.

A life reclaimed

A beautiful story of forgiveness is found in John's gospel in the New Testament. John tells us about a woman who was "caught in the very act of adultery" and was brought before Jesus.

I imagine it this way—

With a vicious shove the men pushed the woman to the ground. She fell into the dirt, her head uncovered, her hair disheveled, a heap of misery. The taunting continued mercilessly as they pulled her to her feet to stand in front of all those who had gathered in the temple porch area listening to Jesus of Nazareth, one of the popular teachers.

She looked around at the men who had dragged her to the temple. Upright leaders like these are above criticism, but I am worthless. I deserve to die, she thought and hung her head in shame. But where was the man who was found in bed with me? she wondered bitterly. After all, there were two of us caught in adultery.

A crowd began to gather around them, to see what was happening, when one of the leaders shouted to Jesus, who was nearby.

"Teacher, this woman was caught in the very act of committing adultery. Now in the law Moses commanded us to stone such women. Now what do you say?"

Jesus didn't answer.

Barely moving her head, she glanced at the teacher and saw him bend down and draw in the dirt with his finger. When the leaders continued to pelt him with questions he rose slowly and said, "Let anyone among you who is without sin be the first to throw a stone at her." And he knelt down and drew in the dirt again.

She braced herself against the inevitable pain to come, squeezing her eyes tightly shut. She heard the shuffling of feet and knew they were preparing to haul her out to the place at the edge of town where public stonings took place. Large rocks would be hurled at her, battering her body until she no longer could breathe.

If fortune smiles on me, she reasoned, an early stone will take consciousness from me and I will not feel the slow torture of my flesh being torn from my bones. Then her thoughts turned to her family and what shame they would bear.

Authentic Forgiving: Offering Forgiveness and Grace

She waited—but instead of being pushed and shoved out of the Temple grounds, she became aware of the noise lessening, and then it was quiet.

Hesitantly, she opened her eyes and looked into the most compassionate gaze she had ever seen.

"Woman, where are they?" the teacher asked. "Has no one condemned you?"

She looked around but saw none of the men who had dragged her to the temple. Even the crowd that had gathered around her had moved back and were eyeing them quizzically.

"No one, sir," she said cautiously, still fearing what her fate would be.

Then she heard the words that would transform her life forever.

"Neither do I condemn you. Go your way, and from now on do not sin again."

(Story based on John 8:2-11)

Can you imagine the awe mixed with relief when this woman realized her life had been given back to her by this rabbi who seemed to care more about people than laws, one who stood up to the religious leaders who would have had her stoned to death?

Jesus did not condone her sin, but neither did he condemn her. Her life was restored, with an admonition to change directions, to become a new creation. Jesus was in the business of renewal.

He still is.

Are you in need of re-creation today? Is your sin too big for God to forgive? Have you sinned too many times for God to forgive you? Are your sins too great for God to forgive you? Is your life so messed up that there's no hope of being reconciled to God and receiving his unreserved love?

No! On all counts, no! Not according to the Bible. 1 John 1:9 says, "If we confess our sins, he is faithful and just and will forgive us our sins and purify us from all unrighteousness."

In her book, *Knowing God*, Kim Reisman explains it like this: "Experiencing God's grace, restoring our friendship with God, begins when we recognize our sinfulness, earnestly repent, and accept the forgiveness God offers us through Jesus Christ. The grace we experience, referred to as justifying grace, is the redemptive, healing, recreating love of God..."[33]

The redemptive love of God

One of my favorite verses (I have many!) is Isaiah 43:1b. "Fear not, for I have redeemed you; I have summoned you by name; you are mine."

God calls us to him by name, not just a generic, "Hey, Everybody, step this way." But a personal call to each of us. Do you hear it?

I can imagine God saying to you, "Beloved, I have created you for great things. Come, follow my perfect plan for your life. You are redeemed."

I love reflecting on the concept of *redemption*. I adore the sound of the word *redeemed*. I sing to the rafters the old hymn, *"Redeemed, how I love to proclaim it."*

I learned the meaning of the word "redemption" when I was just a child. It was my job to paste into the provided books, the S&H Green Stamps given to us as incentives at our local grocery store. After attaching the stamps, I would count

---

[33] Kimberly Dunnam Reisman, *Knowing God: Making God the Main Thing in My Life* (Nashville, TN: Abingdon Press, 2003), 52.

how many books we had accumulated, then study the redemption catalog to see what we could get in exchange for them—a toaster, silver place settings, pots and pans—all kinds of valuable objects were available.

We could accumulate quite a pile of stamp books, but they were worthless to us if we didn't take them to the redemption center and exchange them for the items of value.

Too often we are burdened with feelings of worthlessness because of sin in our lives. And all the while God is inviting us to come to the redemption center—to come to him to exchange our old life for a new one—to be forgiven and released from the pain of our sin. When we do, we give God our old lives and begin to recognize our immense value in his kingdom. God's redemption transforms us into women of unlimited potential.

Restoration—at the end of the road, home

You may know the story of the prodigal son which was told by Jesus and recorded in the book of Luke: A young man was fed up with living at home and asked his father to give him his inheritance so he could leave and be on his own. (Young people rebelling against parents is not new, evidently.) He "set off for a distant country and there squandered his wealth in wild living." Luke 15:13

It wasn't long before his whole inheritance was spent. When a famine hit the land where he was living, the young man was reduced to feeding pigs. No doubt those listening to Jesus telling the story were horrified that this young Jewish man was having anything to do with pigs.

"When he came to his senses, he said, 'How many of my father's hired men have food to spare, and here I am starving to death! I will set out and go back to my father and say to him: Father, I have sinned against heaven and against you. I am no longer worthy to be called your son; make me like one of your hired men.' So he got up and went to his father." Luke 15:17-20a

Meanwhile the father had waited every day, hoping that his errant son would return. I can imagine that every time the father went outside, he'd look down the road to see if his boy was returning.

Then one day he saw a figure in the distance that looked like it could be his son. The father's heart must have skipped a beat while he watched. As the dusty traveler came closer, the father threw down the things he was carrying and ran with open arms to meet his son.

The father had already forgiven his son, even before being asked to do so. But the son had to return home before he could know about and accept that forgiveness.

Often we're afraid to "go home." We try to become good enough before turning to God, or we don't believe God will forgive us. Like the prodigal son, we must return home—must turn toward God—before we can see that God's loving arms are reaching out to embrace us.

When we believe that God loves us unconditionally, we, in turn, can learn to forgive others. It's not always easy, but that's where spiritual growth comes in—the subject of our next chapter.

ACTION STEPS:
Questions to Consider on Forgiveness

Writing in your journal or using some other method can help you think through the concept of forgiveness and how it needs to be a part of your life.

Authentic Forgiving: Offering Forgiveness and Grace

Forgiving Others—
1. Who in your past or present has hurt you in some way big or small? A parent, ex-spouse, sibling, child, co-worker, boss, friend, ex-friend?
2. Is it possible to talk with this person about reconciliation without making the situation worse? Why or why not?
3. If it seems possible to reconcile with the other person, pray before, during and after the attempt.
4. Sometimes it's better to move on without dealing directly with the person who has hurt you. If that's the case, record how you will do this, turning the situation over to God and trusting him to help you heal.
5. Are you harboring resentments that are of your own making? Have you blown out of proportion slights or comments made by others? If you are hurt easily by what others say

Some thoughts on forgiveness—

- Forgiveness is not condoning the wrong someone has done to you, but releasing resentment and hatred to free your heart for positive living.
- We hear of holding a grudge or nursing a grudge. Instead, we can ask God to take away the grudge or resentment we feel, so we are not held captive by the very thing we are trying to hold on to.

when you know they don't mean to hurt you, ask God to help you properly interpret what others say.
6. Has someone asked for your forgiveness but you have not been willing to forgive?

Accepting Forgiveness—
1. In what situations do you need to accept forgiveness?
2. Do you have trouble forgiving yourself for something you've done?
3. Has someone offered forgiveness but you can't let go of the wrong you did? Ask God to heal that incident.
4. Do you have trouble believing that God can completely forgive you for things you've done?
5. Do you need to confess sins and ask for forgiveness?
6. Seek the assistance of a friend, counselor, pastor or other helper if you need help with these issues.
7. You may find it helpful to commit to memory the following verse:

- Lack of forgiveness is sometimes a result of wanting a sense of control over someone who has hurt us. However, the one who doesn't forgive continues to be held in the grip of the pain.
- Forgiving others and accepting forgiveness frees us to soar and become the authentic, influential women we were created to be.

"Have mercy on me, O God, according to your unfailing love; according to your great compassion blot out my transgressions. Wash away all my iniquity and cleanse me from my sin." Psalm 51:1-2

- Psalm 103:8 tells us, "The LORD is compassionate and gracious, slow to anger, abounding in love." Ask God for a compassionate heart so that you can "abound in love."

CHAPTER FIVE
Authentic Growing: Moving from mediocre to marvelous

"For we are God's workmanship, created in Christ Jesus to do good works, which God prepared in advance for us to do."

Ephesians 2:10

Because we are created in the image of God, we need to honor that reality by always growing and reflecting God's magnificence to the best of our ability. We seek excellence, not because God needs our endorsement, but because we already have his.

Yet, too often we doubt that God could use us in special ways. We are content to "play it safe," doing life as we've always done it.

In *Knowing God*, Kimberly Reisman says:

God never sees us in the same way we see ourselves. Nor does God see us as the world sees us. We may see ourselves as unacceptable, or maybe just exceedingly ordinary; the world may see us that way as well. But God never sees us as mundane, never as unacceptable. The person God sees is unique and loved and always named as a beloved child.[34]

I've been told that the Greek word used for "workmanship" in Ephesians 2:10 is "poiema," from which our English word "poem" is derived. Isn't that an amazing thought—that we are God's poem!

We dare not think of ourselves as mediocre and suited only for mundane living when God has written a marvelous script for our lives, if only we will follow it.

Growing into greatness

What would happen if we broke through our self-imposed barriers and dared to live intentionally? How would life change for us? Would we create a "new normal"?

Changing our status quo means changing ourselves in the process.

In Chapter Three we talked about how limiting it is when we let someone else tell us who we are. We stay at a level of mediocrity when we allow low self-esteem to define us, and when we don't believe that God wants to use us in amazing ways. However, we can accomplish all God calls us to do when we realize that we are created for greatness and when we are willing to grow into that greatness. God calls us and equips us. We can become proficient in whatever he wills for us to do.

Longing for significance

When our children were in Middle School, Sunday night after church was game time at our house. It was a good-natured,

---

[34] Kimberly Dunnam Reisman, *Knowing God: Making God the Main Thing in My Life* (Nashville, TN: Abingdon Press, 2003), 63.

noisy, bonding time for all of us. One of our favorite games was Trivial Pursuit™. It was amazing how much generally useless information we each possessed! We were pretty evenly matched, two adults against two young teenagers.

Those game nights were great fun, but I don't want to play "trivial pursuit" with my life. I'm not content to collect the tiny pieces of life's trivial pursuit pie. I am not satisfied with the status quo. Are you? Or do you feel a restlessness and wonder why and what you can do about it?

Ron Hutchcraft, in *Called to Greatness*, says, "Our 'sick and tired of the status quo' feelings are actually a magnet drawing us toward the greater greatness for which we were created. Our restlessness is actually a *holy discontentment*. In fact, it is likely that God has made you restless!"[35]

That idea needs to get our attention. We can tune in to our bodies, minds and hearts and listen carefully when we are not content. Perhaps it is indeed a Godly discontentment that is calling to us. We may not be called to *do* more, but to *be* more—to be more loving, to be more patient, to be more forgiving, to be more like Christ.

A few years ago I was interviewed on Erin Campbell's radio program, "Water Through the Word." At the end of her interviews Erin adds recordings of her speaking encouraging words over the soothing sounds of music. She has several of these scripture medleys with different themes and asked me which one I would like played after my interview. At first I thought I wanted, "You Are Loved," because that is a message I want every woman to hear and take to heart. But after thinking it over, I chose, "You Are Significant," and then wondered why that one

---

35   Ron Hutchcraft, *Called to Greatness* (Chicago: Moody Publishers, 2004), 17.

had appealed to me so strongly. Pondering that decision gave me new insight into my own desires. That sense of wanting "significance" was not because I needed to feel important, and I wasn't seeking praise, I simply wanted to make my life count for something beyond my own small day-to-day activities.

I'm seeing this same idea expressed around the world, in both Christian and secular circles. In spite of difficult economic times, in many areas there is a spirit of hope and possibility. There seems to be a surge of longing for significance, making life count, not out of fear of God's wrath, but out of gratitude and a desire to make something meaningful of our lives.

"There is in every human soul," says Hutchcraft, "the need to be part of something much bigger than any earth achievement, or even any earth relationship, can offer. We aspire to a life of *greatness, lasting* greatness."[36]

But how do we move from mediocre to marvelous? How do we experience lives of significance? God invites us to grow up, to become emotionally, relationally and spiritually mature.

Let's look at a few ways we can grow into the persons God had in mind when we were created. Each of these growth topics could easily be a book in itself, but we'll touch on each of the three, emotional, relational and spiritual, with some ideas that can help you begin the process.

Emotional Growth

The importance of emotional health cannot be overlooked if we want to become the fully-developed persons God has in mind for us to be. In addition to having a strong sense of self-worth, as we talked about in Chapter Three, another aspect to consider is our emotional intelligence. Several books have been

---

36   Ibid., 16.

published in the last ten years on this subject, helping us to understand the importance of being aware of our emotions and the emotions of those people around us. This knowledge allows us to have healthier relationships at home and at work.

Dr. Laura Belsten says, "Each day in our personal and professional lives opportunities and challenges present themselves, and it is emotional intelligence that enables us to recognize and move towards those opportunities as well as rise above life's challenges."[37]

Emotional intelligence involves self management and relationship management as well as self-awareness and awareness of others. One aspect of this is concerned with reactions during stress. Knowing how we react in times of stress helps us to manage our emotions and relate to others in constructive ways. That is true whether the stress is due to something like the loss of a job or dealing with a teething toddler. We will have stress. How we react to that stress is up to us to decide. By knowing what our natural tendencies are, we can decide to change our behavior if that would be beneficial. We do not have to be held captive to our natural tendencies.

One way to do this is to replace unwanted anger and negative feelings by re-thinking our situation and concentrating on the blessings we have in our lives. This is not to say we should cover up our feelings and pretend to feel differently. Letting our emotions go "underground" is not healthy. But actually learning to appropriately show our emotions, rather than "losing it," creating further problems for ourselves and those around us, can be much healthier. The subject is much too extensive for us to go into very deeply here, but if you feel emotional intelligence

---

37   Laura Belsten, Ph.D., *Coaching Emotional Intelligence* (Boulder, Colorado: LearnMore Communications, Inc., 2006), 5.

is something that would help you be more authentically successful in life, you might consider studying more about it on your own or with a coach or counselor.

We can help our emotional health by taking care of our physical health. When we eat right, sleep well, exercise our bodies, recreate, laugh, relax, take time to be quiet, spend time with friends and family in fun ways, and exercise our brains by learning new things, our emotional health as well as our general health is improved.

Growing in Relationships

We are created for community, although we express this need in different ways. For some people it means having lots of people around all the time, the more the merrier, the louder the better. Others prefer one-on-one interactions in quiet settings. Whatever our preference, it is important to take care of relationships and help them grow in healthy ways.

Dr. Gary Chapman in his book, *The Five Love Languages*, tells us that we perceive love in different ways. Understanding how someone perceives love allows you to better meet that need in their lives. Whether you are dealing with a spouse, children, parents, siblings, friends, or colleagues, you can create healthier relationships by learning to speak in a language they understand. And by understanding your own "love language" you can see why you respond to some overtures and not to others, even though they were intended to show you love.

Which of these looks like something you would react most positively to?

Words of Affirmation
Quality Time
Receiving Gifts

Acts of Service

Physical Touch

Of course, most of us will want each of these at appropriate times, but one may stand out as being needed more often than the others.

I have a confession to make. I very seldom pump my own gasoline. It's messy and smelly and awkward, and I just don't like to do it. I don't remember when it started, but somewhere along the line, during our forty years of wedded bliss, my hubby started making sure there was always gas in the tank when I would be going out without him. (Yes, that's one reason why I proudly wear my black velour baseball cap with "Spoiled Rotten" spelled out in crystals.) At our house we say that my love language is having someone fill up the gas tank.

We can laugh at that love language. But some disconnects are tragic.

I vividly remember a young woman I knew many years ago whose husband had become very "successful" in business and showered her with gifts, including a huge diamond solitaire ring. When a friend of mine remarked to her what a beautiful ring it was, the unhappy woman replied, "Here, do you want it? It means nothing to me." That marriage was in serious peril. While the husband was trying to show his love through gifts, his wife wasn't getting the message. She may have needed time and affection from him while he was spending long hours at work to be able to shower her with gifts.

We talked in Chapter One about the importance of understanding our personalities and temperaments. Here again, by being knowledgeable about ourselves and those we communicate with, we can enhance our relationships. Just treating others the way we would like to be treated is not enough. They may not be able to interpret our language. We must learn what the needs of our loved ones are and try to meet those needs.

Growing in Spiritual Development

How do we grow spiritually? John Ortberg, in his book, *The Life You've Always Wanted*, says, "Spiritual growth is a molding process: We are to be to Christ as an image is to the original."[38]

Being a grandmother, I have a lot of experience with Play-doh™. And I can tell you that it's impossible to mold and shape this compound if it has become dry and stiff. I make sure the jars are kept tightly closed to hold in the moisture, so when the two grand-princesses come over for a visit and want to create triangles, squares, frogs and flowers, the dough will be soft and malleable.

We need also to give our hearts appropriate care so they are malleable. By harboring anger and resentment or by living as if we are in charge and don't need Godly assistance, we can become hard-hearted and unable to be molded into the image of the Christ.

Jeremiah 24:7 reminds us, "I will give them a heart to know me, that I am the LORD. They will be my people, and I will be their God, for they will return to me with all their heart."

God will give us such a heart if we are open to receiving it and if we carve out quiet times to hear God speak.

So, our prayer must be like that of the Psalmist who said: "Teach us to number our days aright, that we may gain a heart of wisdom." Psalm 90:12

---

[38] John Ortberg, *The Life You've Always Wanted: spiritual disciplines for ordinary people* (Grand Rapids, Michigan: Zondervan, 2002), 20.

Spiritual types

In her book, *Discover Your Spiritual Type,* Dr. Corinne Ware addresses the difficulty some people have with experiencing anything of a spiritual nature.

"One is not likely to have an experience of the Holy if one believes it not possible to do so. We can do only what we can first imagine. The much discussed Western poverty of spirit may not be so much a consequence of accelerated knowledge as it is a dearth of imagination. Unlike Jesus, we live as orphans without a spiritual story."[39]

But for those who want to grow spiritually, those who *can* imagine experiencing the Holy, they still may experience stumbling blocks. Some women feel out of sync in religious gatherings of various types and don't know why. In our desire for certain worship styles and personal times with God, we may wonder if we're doing it "right." And many people will be glad to tell us that their way is the only way to do it!

We know that we have personality differences and different emotional intelligences, but what about different spiritual types?

I began to understand why I felt more connected to God in some settings than in others after reading Dr. Ware's book. She examines spiritual types and how they relate to different forms of worship.

For the person who has primarily an intellectual spirituality, those things she can "see, touch, and vividly imagine" will be important. "Their choices will be based mostly on activity and on corporate gathering: more study groups, better sermons,

---

39   Dr. Corinne Ware, *Discover Your Spiritual Type: a guide to individual and congregational growth (Bethesda, Maryland: The Alban Institute, 1995),* 21.

and some sort of theological renewal within the worshipping community."[40]

Dr. Ware describes the next type as being heart rather than head spirituality, saying, "A type 2 will characteristically emphasize evangelism, since experience must be shared, and on transformation, sometimes of an obvious, even sudden type. Witnessing, testimonials, and especially music mark corporate worship."[41]

Type 3, according to Dr. Ware, is a Mystic Spirituality. For this person God is seen as "ineffable, unnameable, and more vast than any known category...a life of austerity and asceticism is appealing to many in this quadrant."[42]

The fourth type is "an active visionary who is single-minded with a deeply focused almost crusading type of spirituality."[43]

Dr. Ware points out that each of us will recognize more than one type within our own makeup but will probably have a strong affinity toward one type.

After only a cursory look at spiritual types we can see that people with such varied approaches to spirituality will likely want to worship in ways related to their type and may feel out of touch with other worship styles. One person prefers quiet, reverent contemplation, perhaps with a sense of the mysterious, while another chooses a more kinesthetic approach, wanting active praise movements and joyous singing.

The dangers we face are either in thinking that we are not spiritual enough because we don't fit what we see around us, or if we have a good fit, that a different form and type is less spiritual than the one we enjoy.

40	Ibid., 37.
41	Ibid., 39.
42	Ibid., 41.
43	Ibid., 43.

With knowledge of spiritual types we can begin to understand ourselves and others and learn to give room for more than one way of relating to God, all still within the traditional Christian understanding of spiritual growth.

Change your mind so you can change your life.

In spite of being able to understand ourselves and others better, we will still experience life at a diminished level if we have not been able to let go of negative self-talk.

Why do so many Christians suffer defeatist attitudes when the Bible tells us to think positively, give up our fears and depend on God? Could it be that we're not believing and claiming God's promises? We're not telling ourselves what God has already told us.

Often, in our search for answers, we overlook what the Bible says and look for something "new." We hear a lot these days about positive thinking and possibility thinking from secular success gurus. They promise abundance, high self-esteem and unlimited success—usually if we buy their products—but this is not a new teaching. The things many of them are saying are the same things the Bible has said, but couched in different terminology. Yet, we get excited about this "new teaching" and fail to recognize the true source.

It reminds me of how excited little children get when they discover for the first time how family members are related.

"Mom! Did you know Uncle Mike is your brother!" We smile and realize the child has some growing and learning ahead of him.

Chuck Swindoll nails it when he says, "I'm sure it comes as no surprise to most of us that we act out precisely what we take in. In other words, we become what we think. Long before that familiar line found its way into Psychology 101 and hyped-up sales meetings, the Bible included it in one of its ancient scrolls; it just said it in a little different way: 'For as he thinks within himself, so he is' (Prov. 23:7)" [44]

It's a Biblical concept to make sure our thoughts are harnessed and focused on good things. Our self-talk must be positive and uplifting, if we want to move from mediocrity to marvelous.

"Finally, brothers, whatever is true, whatever is noble, whatever is right, whatever is pure, whatever is lovely, whatever is admirable—if anything is excellent or praiseworthy—think about such things." Philippians 4:8

Swindoll goes on to say, "Let me get to the heart of the issue. Since the mind holds the secrets of soaring, the enemy of our souls has made the human mind the bull's-eye of his target. His most insidious and strategic moves are made upon the mind. By affecting the way we think, he is able to keep our lives on a mediocre level."[45]

Instead of soaring like eagles, we shuffle around, heads down, pecking at whatever grain we happen to find on the ground. We're afraid to leave what we already know. We're afraid of change. We may wish to make progress, but we want to hold on to what is familiar with one hand, while reaching tentatively out with the other to feel our way into the future.

This can be a good strategy to some degree. We need not to jump hastily at every "bright shiny object" that attracts our attention. But carried to extremes, it can pull us apart. We're not successful in either camp if we try to keep one hand in the past and one in the future. In Chapter Eight we'll look closer

---

44 Charles R. Swindoll, *Living Above the Level of Mediocrity: a Commitment to Excellence* (Waco, Texas: Word Books, 1987), 19.
45 Ibid., 21.

at how we react to change and how we can move through the stages that come with change.

Another key to moving from mediocre to marvelous is to live intentionally. Blaming someone else for our situation, waiting for change to happen externally, or wanting a Knight in Shining Armor to appear and rescue us from our status quo existence are all counterproductive approaches.

God calls us to step out of our comfort zones and promises us, like he did Joshua when he was called to lead the Israelites into the Promised Land, that we are not alone in our journey. God will be with us.

"Have I not commanded you? Be strong and courageous. Do not be terrified; do not be discouraged, for the LORD your God will be with you wherever you go." Joshua 1:9

I recently taught a class on making decisions that I called, "Live with Courage—Lead with Confidence: A Plan for Living Courageously in Troubling Times"

Here are the six steps for implementing that plan:

1. Focus on God and His plan for your life. I return again and again to Jeremiah 29:11 because it reminds me that God does have a plan for my life—and it's the best plan!

2. Trust that God has control over the things you don't—although situations may not unfold the way you want them to.

When we let go of our anxiety about tomorrow, when we remember the lilies of the field and see ourselves as fellow-occupants of God's great garden, when we are not so busy trying to make things happen that we forget about God, he can work in our lives. ("Consider how the lilies grow. They do not labor or spin. Yet I tell you, not even Solomon in all his splendor was dressed like one of these." Luke 12:27)

3. Put things in perspective—just how bad is it? Victor Frankl, in *Man's Search for Meaning*, shares the secret he discovered as a prisoner in a German concentration camp during World War II. He says there's only one thing that cannot be taken from us—our attitude. It is likely that we will never be in such dire circumstances as Frankl, yet we can learn from his experience. We can be aware of our attitude in all things and choose to focus on our blessings.

4. Be pro-active in assessing the situation to decide the best direction to go. Don't wait for someone else to come in and tell you what you need to do. Ask God to reveal it to you. Then listen.

Sometimes, though, we don't get a clear answer. At that time we may need to just get up and do something. We can become paralyzed by thinking too much and worrying that our solution won't be the perfect one. By actually taking a first step, our brains seem to move into a higher gear, and we are able to think more clearly about what the second step should be.

5. Give the results to God. When we've asked for God's direction, then taken the steps to move down that path—to the best of our abilities—we need to rest in God's peace. We are loved by the Creator and even if we make a mistake, he will not leave us, but will guide us back to the right path.

6. *Repeat from Step #1.* We must continually go back and begin the cycle again because new challenges will come our way or we take back the problem that we thought we had turned over to God.

Nurturing atmosphere—
As a community of faith, Christians can help one another in this challenge to grow into the persons we were created to be.

Rather than looking at others critically (so we can feel better about ourselves, perhaps?), we are to nurture one another and exhort one another to excel, if we are to experience optimal growth.

"The proper nourishment for personal growth is a loving acceptance and encouragement by others, not rejection and impatient suggestions for improvement. Human beings, like plants, grow in the soil of acceptance, not in the atmosphere of rejection…there is in most of us a civil war that stunts our personal growth. It is our inner struggle for self-acceptance,"[46] say John Powell and Loretta Brady in their book, *Will the Real Me Please Stand Up?*

As married couples, we are to nurture our spouses. As parents, we are to nurture our children. As church members, we are to nurture our fellow believers. As world citizens, we are to nurture anyone God puts in our path.

In a society whose favorite pastimes seem to be to criticize and complain, we can indeed be beacons of light wherever we are, at work or play. We can learn to nurture and nourish those with whom we connect. When we do, we not only help others, but we help ourselves to grow.

Stretching and soaring

Over the double doors leading from my bedroom is a glass transom with etched images of butterflies and hummingbirds. Both are symbols of new life and resurrection. Each morning as I go out to meet the day, I see those images and am reminded that it's a fresh day with new and exciting possibilities. It's a

---

[46] John Powell, S.J. and Loretta Brady, M.S.W., *Will the Real Me Please Stand Up?* (Allen, Texas: Resources for Christian Living, 1985), 94.

day with the capacity for growth and transformation, if I'm willing to take the risk.

When we could be unfurling our wings and soaring effortlessly, we cling to the familiar, crawling like caterpillars, holding on fiercely lest we fall from our tree branch. Or we inch slowly along the ground, not even realizing there's more to life—that we were created to experience a wider world.

Once we are able to move beyond the status quo and grow emotionally, relationally and spiritually, we are able to dream big dreams and be used by God in remarkable ways. In the next chapter, we'll explore how to generate new dreams and rekindle forgotten ones so we can live authentically.

What is your big dream?

> **Steps to positive growth**
>
> If we are to change and grow,
>
> we must have a desire to do so,
>
> we must realize that it is possible,
>
> we must recognize and define the challenge set before us,
>
> we must take action.
>
> In order to change and grow we must acknowledge what is, accept what isn't and anticipate what can be.

ACTION STEPS:

Look at the following topics and see which ones resonate with you. If you have been journaling or want to start now, write your thoughts on each idea that speaks to you in some way. How can your observations help you grow?

Some Obstacles That Keep Us from Growing—
Fear of change
Not recognizing the need for growth
Not understanding our capacity for growth
Being comfortable with the status quo
Not knowing where to begin
Not taking time to contemplate and reflect
Not recognizing opportunity in adversity

Chapter Six
Authentic Dreaming: Learning to dream again—asking God for the vision

"In the last days, God says, I will pour out my Spirit on all people. Your sons and daughters will prophesy, your young men will see visions, your old men will dream dreams."

Acts 2:17

It's time to dream big dreams. *Really* big dreams.

By tapping into your dreams, you share your God-given abilities with others who in turn use their gifts to bless even more people. The ripple effect creates untold blessings that literally can reach around the world.

John Maxwell, in *Success 101*, says:

> Without a dream, we may struggle to see potential in ourselves because we don't look beyond our current circumstances. But with a dream, we begin to see ourselves in a new light, as having greater potential

and being capable of stretching and growing to reach it.[47]

In order to move forward, we need to let go of those dreams which are no longer valid, re-embrace past ideas that still have merit, and explore the new visions that have developed as we have matured.

As a child you may have dreamed of becoming a ballet dancer, a minister, an astronaut, a teacher, a missionary, a doctor, or any number of other professionals. Sometimes such dreams are realized without a glitch, but perhaps that didn't happen for you. Life may have gotten in the way of your most cherished dreams. You may have gotten sidetracked by bad decisions or circumstances that were truly beyond your control. What seemed like a good career idea at the time may have lost its lustre. Or possibly you weren't brave enough to attempt what you really wanted to do. Have you hidden your dreams for so long you don't know where they are? It's time to find them, dust them off and re-evaluate them.

Some of our dreams may fall into the category of goals to be attained and challenges to overcome, while others are life-changing, kingdom-building movements. Both are honorable and may be important at different phases of your life and are worth looking at to see if they need to be revived.

You may have outgrown a childish dream, realizing you would not really be fitted for such an occupation. Wanting to grow up to be a professional football player when you turned out to be a 115-pound, 4' 11" adult, may not look as enticing as it did when you were five years old—even for a women's

---

[47] John Maxwell, *Success 101* (Nashville, Tennessee: Thomas Nelson, 2008), 19.

football league. That kind of dream is easy to let go of. What's harder is giving up the dream of being someone you think you could have been if you had just had the opportunity. You may need to adjust the focus of your dream.

For instance, if you're forty and always wanted to be a concert violinist, but you've never learned to play any instrument, you may not make it to Carnegie Hall as a soloist, but you may indeed learn to play the instrument well enough to enjoy it. And who knows, you could have a chance to perform in Carnegie Hall as a member of an ensemble. Stranger things have happened. I have had the thrill of singing in Carnegie Hall as a member of a large chorus which helped to cover up any less than dulcet tones!

So, some dreams should be allowed to die peacefully, others can be altered to fit present circumstances, and still others are new and fresh and created for the future. As you have experienced life and learned many skills, you probably feel drawn to explore new directions. Out of the most difficult events in your life, you may have gained strength, and you now have compassion for and want to help others going through similar experiences. You have a vision of how God can redeem your pain by helping others.

Dreamers and Visionaries

Is there a difference between being a dreamer and a visionary?

"To dream" sounds, well, *dreamy*, not too solid—ephemeral. By contrast, "to have vision" indicates a take-charge, forward moving action.

For our purposes, we will use the terms interchangeably. So when I speak of dreams and dreaming, it is with a sense of examining the big ideas we have been given and anticipating how God is speaking to us about those ideas. At some point, of course, we need to move from idle dreaming to committed action, which we might think of as carrying out the vision.

So how do we go about dreaming and visioning? Where do we start?

We can begin by carving out some time to think about those things we would like to do—maybe something we've wanted to do for a long time but didn't think we could.

First state the dream. (*I want to write a book and get it published.*) Then move to a vision of what it will take to make that happen. (*I'll attend writers' conferences and pitch my ideas to publishers.*) Finally, it's good to envision what the results will look like. (*I will receive the Pulitzer Prize for*...oops, I got carried away there for a minute...but maybe that's okay while I'm dreaming.)

I suppose I've always been a dreamer. My teachers usually didn't appreciate that splendid quality. Day-dreaming looks an awful lot like procrastinating and wasting time. But I've learned that it can be useful and can re-energize our lives. It's okay to set aside time for contemplation, meditation, reflection, observation, rumination, pondering, musing...dreaming!

In our rush-about world, we find it hard to step outside of the hustle and bustle to listen to our own heartbeat and to hear the voice of God. In Chapter Two we talked about the importance of learning to listen. This is a good time to put that skill to work. It's also useful to have pen and paper handy to write down thoughts and reflections. What ideas and questions bubble up for you when you take time to ask your heart what you should be doing at this stage of your life?

Ask yourself the deep questions that will move you forward in re-awakening your dream. Let your mind roam freely. Don't put the brakes on before you get a chance to dream big dreams.

Authentic Dreaming: Learning to dream again

What do you *really* want to do? What do you feel God is calling you to? What are you passionate about? What is the transformation you want to experience in your life, your family, or your work? And very important: What do you need to let go of in order to have what you want?

I find that many women have trouble doing this. They have put others' desires ahead of their own for so long that they really don't know what they want. They lack purpose and don't know how to go about finding it.

As mentioned in Chapter Two, ask yourself what keeps you awake at night? What local or world problem continues to trouble you? What do you find yourself praying for again and again? Answers to these questions will help you understand what you are most passionate about.

Some other helpful questions are: What are you happiest doing? What do you look forward to?

Frederick Buechner has said, "The place God calls you to is the place where your deep gladness and the world's deep hunger meet."[48]

Self-limiting beliefs

While allowing our dreams to surface, it's very important to use what we learned in previous chapters about positive self-talk. It's easy to squelch a dream before it's fully formed by listening to the internal grinches that try to hold us back.

Many times we limit ourselves by thinking we can't do something because we've never done it before, or we just don't have time to do what we'd really like to do. Be realistic about your present obligations, but don't be fooled into thinking

---

[48] Buechner, Frederick. *Wishful Thinking: A Theological ABC*. (San Francisco: HarperSanFrancisco, 1993), 95.

you can't do things differently and in a much bigger way than you've been accustomed to doing.

Andy Stanley reminds us, "From the outset, just about every God-ordained vision appears to be impossible."[49]

As we learned in Chapter Three, you're not too old, too young, too plump, too thin, too poor, too wealthy, too shy, too outgoing to do what God has gifted you to do. So if any of these or other negative thoughts work their way into your thinking, banish them immediately. Replace them with the truth: *"I can do whatever God calls me to do."*

Let God help you think beyond your own abilities to what he will help you become. When you have a big dream but you're hesitant to go for it, try to identify what is holding you back. Is it fear of failure, feelings of inadequacy or an inability to see how God can use you? After you have identified what you feel God would have you do and named the fear that's holding you back, then move boldly through the fear by taking the first step—in spite of your fear. That first step will lead to the next one and then the one after that, until you are well along the path of becoming the woman God had in mind all along.

I believe strongly that it's never too late to dream and follow God's path for your life. I haven't seen a retirement plan yet for kingdom work, so I suggest we carry on until one comes along. Indeed, if we take Old Testament characters such as Abraham and Sarah as role models, we'd better take good care of our bodies, because we have many years of usefulness ahead!

---

49   Andy Stanley, *Visioneering* (Sisters, Oregon: Multnomah Publishers, Inc., 1999), 41.

Discernment and timing

Be sure you're dreaming your own—and God's—dream. Don't let someone else tell you what your dream should be. Some people may try to discourage you from following your dreams, either to protect you from what they think might not be successful for you or because the change threatens them in some way. Surround yourself with Godly people who will support you as you seek God's will. Find someone who will believe in you and your dream even on those days when you can't believe it for yourself.

Several years ago I stepped way out of my comfort zone at a motivational seminar and broke a board, karate style. Producing that whack proved to *me* I could do it. The instructor already knew I could do it. He said so. My compatriots believed I could do it. They said so. Then they gathered around me and started chanting, *"Go, go, go…"* until in a feverish pitch they willed my hand right through the board. It actually felt like a group effort, even though I was the one demolishing the board.

I keep that broken board to remind me that alone I am weak, but with the proper help, I can do more than I thought possible.

How about you? Do you have a person or a group who prays with and for you, holding your dream before you when your vision gets weak?

What an awesome privilege and responsibility we have in the community of faith to nurture and encourage. Supporting one another in our God-given dreams can build up the Kingdom for all of us as we encourage each other to dream even bigger than we could alone. We can pray for the dreams others hold—for discernment, perseverance and right timing.

I love what Ann Platz says in her book, *Reclaiming Your Dream: Awaken Hope and Realize Your Destiny*. "We limit ourselves when we do not allow God to do the dreaming. His dreams are so much bigger and better than ours. He is the Maker of Dreams and the Keeper of Dreams, and He will hold them in reserve until the time is right to fulfill them."[50]

What a great thought—that God will hold our dreams in reserve for us if this isn't the right time for them to be fulfilled. Sometimes when I'm coaching, a client will talk about all she would like to do, but because she has young children she can't, and she's extremely frustrated. I encourage her to relax, ask God what is most important for her to do presently, and trust him to show her when it's time for the dream held in reserve. All in God's good timing.

"We dream of the touch on our shoulder that will call us to greatness, to an act that would change the world," says Kent Nerburn. "But the touches on our shoulder call us only to the small acts of everyday life—changing diapers, changing lightbulbs, changing schedules. Far from being exalted beings, we seem to be prisoners of the ordinary, and we are haunted by the insignificance of our days...We must learn to see with other eyes...We must never forget that the mindful practice of daily affairs is also a path into the realm of the spirit."[51]

Do you feel like "a prisoner of the ordinary"? Ask God to give you new eyes and a vision for what your present life can look like.

---

50 Ann Platz, *Reclaiming Your Dream: Awaken Hope and Realize Your Destiny* (Tulsa, Oklahoma: Harrison House, Inc., 2004), 3.

51 Kent Nerburn, *Small Graces: The Quiet Gifts of Everyday Life* (Novato, California: New World Library, 1998) 10, 11.

Perseverance

"If God has birthed a vision in your heart," says Andy Stanley, "the day will come when you will be called upon to make a sacrifice to achieve it. And you will have to make the sacrifice with no guarantee of success."[52]

For instance, if you are a writer you may spend weeks, months and years tapping on a keyboard, not knowing if anyone else will ever read your work. You may feel, like I sometimes do, that maybe it's all just conjured up, sort of like John Nash's work, the Russell Crowe character, in the movie, "A Beautiful Mind."

We create reams and reams of paper splashed with words (like Nash's formulas) that make sense to us, but will they make sense to anyone else? Are we doing important work—or work at all—or are we just filling time and space? Will all this time be spent in vain?

Or maybe you're an entrepreneur, trying to get a business going. You work and work without seeing the success you long for. Just because it's difficult doesn't mean it's not meant to be done. So often the difference between a business succeeding or failing is perseverance—trying just one more time.

Missing the mark

Sometimes God's best plan for us is thwarted by our own willfulness. Ann Platz tells us about her deferred dream:

"...I married the wrong man for all the wrong reasons. I was willful and disobedient. I was outright rebellious!

"When the winds blew, my house came tumbling down. After the marriage failed and my husband deserted me and our two babies, I was so devastated, so wounded, that I wasn't even aware that God's original dream was still intact, just waiting

---

52   Andy Stanley, 114.

to be rediscovered...During this time, however, I learned one lesson well: God still loved me even when I turned away...The dream does not end when you blow it; it is only delayed."[53]

In spite of this rough start to adult life, Ann has become a very successful interior designer, inspirational speaker, author of numerous books, doting grandmother and married a strongly committed Christian man.

She counsels:

> "As your dream comes into fulfillment, as you walk out your destiny, keep loving and forgiving. Let the beauty of Jesus spill out of all your broken places like the perfume in the alabaster box that Mary broke at His feet. Let the sweet aroma of your sacrifice bless all those you meet and mentor. Let your dream carry you to the end with honor and integrity."[54]

Here comes that dreamer!
The Bible is full of stories of people with big dreams. The account of Joseph in the Old Testament is interesting because Joseph's dreams—literal dreams—got him *into trouble* (with his brothers) and *out of trouble* (with the pharaoh).

Joseph wasn't so wise in telling his brothers about some of his dreams. He was young and brash and very possibly a spoiled brat! But God used him in spite of his shortcomings.

Joseph was favored by his father, and his jealous brothers were tired of hearing about his dreams that indicated he would rule over them some day.

---

53   Ann Platz, 6.
54   Ibid., 246.

"Here comes that dreamer!" Joseph's brothers said when they saw him approaching out in the fields where they were shepherding their father's flocks. They first prepared to kill him but ended up throwing him into a pit and then selling him as a slave.

Living as a slave in Egypt, Joseph matured over the years through many hardships and eventually became an assistant to the Pharaoh. His skills at interpreting Pharaoh's dreams resulted in the nation storing plenty of food before a famine hit the land. Because of Joseph's position in Pharaoh's court, he was able to save his family from famine when they came to Egypt hoping to buy food. (From Genesis 37, 39-47)

"Here comes that dreamer!"

May the same be said of us, not because we think more highly of ourselves than we should, of course, but because we dare to dream big, God-sized dreams.

Called to do great things

Don't put limits on God for what you and he can accomplish together.

"Put out into deep water, and let down the nets for a catch," Jesus told Peter, and at first Peter seemed reluctant to do so. After all, he had been fishing all night and caught nothing. "But because you say so," Peter said, "I will let down the nets." (From Luke 5:4-5)

We need to cultivate a "because you say so" mentality. How many blessings do we miss when we assume something can't possibly happen?

"I don't see how I could ever become a doctor—but because you say so, Lord…"

"What could I possibly do about the sex-slave trafficking of young girls around the world? I don't have resources to do anything about that—but because you say so..."

"Start my own business? Surely, you can't mean that, Lord—but because you say so..."

"I'm not nearly talented enough to be an inspirational speaker—but because you say so..."

"I don't see how I could help eradicate world hunger. It's such an immense job—but because you say so..."

"How could we ever afford to adopt a child from overseas—but because you say so..."

Faith and art

Artist Makoto Fujimura in his book, *River Grace*, says God revealed how he wanted to use him as he worked with a mission team, walking the crowded streets of Manila. "God was clearly directing me to a city vision, to think of a way I could contribute, with my art, to the global movement of God's working in the lives of creative individuals. I felt a challenge well up in my heart, 'Think of New York.'...I remember telling my father how I hated New York City. I would visit museums and galleries, of course, but my quiet, introverted nature found the city too aggressive and over-stimulating. So to hear this calling was unnerving. It was not a path I would have chosen on my own."[55]

Fujimura followed this call and moved to New York, but he wondered how he could possibly find representation for his art in New York with so many artists vying for the relatively few

---

55   Makoto Fujimura, *River Grace*, (Self-published by the author, available at www.makotofujimura.com, 2007), 12.

opportunities available, especially since his style did not fit the style of many galleries.

"When Valerie Dillon, the owner of the Dillon Gallery, came for a studio visit, I showed her the screen piece of Twin Rivers #51. She asked me what the gold, smudged writings were, and I answered (taking a deep breath) *'It's from the Bible; from Isaiah 61.'* To this she answered *'Oh, I love Isaiah!'* I am still amazed, after completing numerous solo shows in New York City, that God has provided dealers who appreciate my works from a spiritual perspective."[56]

As a result of his listening to God's call, Fujimura founded The International Arts Movement, creating a bridge from culture to faith using art as a part of "the global movement of God's working in the lives of creative individuals."

Connecting people

When Karen Power, founder of Christian Speakers Services[57] was laid off from her job as a corporate trainer with a Fortune 500 sales training organization, she wondered if this was her opportunity. For many years she had wanted to help Christian speakers and event planners find one another. Previous positions had given her on-the-job-training in many of the skills needed to run this kind of business.

Karen grew up writing and playing gospel music. Several years ago she briefly moved to Nashville to follow her dreams in the music industry, but a downturn in the economy cut that career short. She has said she remembers driving back home and turning the corner into her old neighborhood and thinking, "I'll never get out of this place so I might as well quit

---

56 Ibid., 14.
57 www.ChristianSpeakerServices.com

dreaming about it." But her sister gave her a piece of needlepoint that said, "Never give up on your dreams" and Karen took that sentiment to heart.

Karen shared with me, "It wasn't until the last five years that I realized that all the experiences, both personal and professional, good or bad, were just parts of a tapestry—a bigger picture...during some of the darkest days of my life. I caught a glimpse of the big picture—working with Christian communicators."[58]

Karen is passionate about helping gifted communicators share their messages of hope and healing, through coaching and booking them around the country. "Looking back," she says, "I realize that every step I have taken...and each person that I've met along the way was preparing me for the fulfillment of this dream. When we follow God and pursue His plan for our life, our dreams can come true!"

Living God's best

We need to be sure we are surrendered to God as we are reaching for our dreams. If we are going to be authentic, we must seek what God has created for us. I believe God wants us to use the talents and gifts he has given us and that we can understand our calling best through exploring our gifts, talents and interests. However, sometimes we don't follow God's best path. We hold on to a part of our lives God has asked us to relinquish for our own good. We need to learn the lessons of Moses' calling.

Holding on to second best

In our back gardens we have several euonymus plants known as "Burning Bush." Each autumn they turn a brilliant crimson

---

58   Karen Power, from conversations with the author.

and remind me to stop and listen for the voice of God just as Moses did. It's fitting to have such bushes here since Moses' story is so important to our family.

The first time I heard composer Ken Medema's song, "Moses," my life was changed irrevocably. That was 30 years ago, and every time I've heard it since then, I've been challenged to take inventory. In the song, Medema tells the story of Moses' encounter with God at the burning bush and recounts that God told Moses to throw down his staff. Moses protests at first, yet when he obeys God, he realizes that his staff has become more than it was before. At the end of the song, Medema turns the question to the listener, asking what we might be holding on to and if we're willing to give it up.

God can use us mightily when we give up our tight grip on our lives—our careers, our children, our purses—and let him be in charge. That might even mean giving up one dream for another one that God has in mind—a better one.

We don't understand the paradox of giving up our greatest desires to God in order for him to use our unique talents and gifts. Often those very gifts are used in stronger ways after we have given them up to him. I don't know why this is so, but I do know that it helps us to see where our idols are and whether or not we've let *anything* in our lives become more important than God.

Think big; think really, really big!

Bruce Wilkinson tells about going to South Africa and becoming overwhelmed by the needs of the thousands of children there, orphaned by AIDS. "We had been asking the question 'What can we do?' But it had brought inadequate results. Now we saw that every Dreamer is invited to look at a Big Need through God's eyes, then ask, 'What does God want done?'"[59]

There is so much need in our world, and rather than becoming overwhelmed by what we can't do, we need to ask what our part is in meeting those needs.

Interpreting the dream—

When the time is right we need to go beyond just thinking about our dreams and put feet to them. When we do, several questions arise.

How can we be sure our dream is God's dream? You can become your own life coach and ask important questions that help you dig deeply.

First of all, have you given your life to God and asked him to use you as he desires?

Next, is following through on this dream going to hurt others—husband, children, church, friends, co-workers? God-given dreams are never selfish, what's-in-it-for-me dreams, but instead are ways of using your talents and abilities to enrich the lives of others as well as yourself. (I don't mean that you should never do things that meet your own needs. An indulgent trip to the local spa periodically may be just what you need to be able to take on the needs of your family and community. Appropriate self-care is crucial to becoming the woman you were created to be. God ordained a time for rest, remember?)

Does your dream line up with scripture? A God-given dream will never contradict God's word. Find a good study Bible, or get help from a friend or pastor if you don't have much Bible knowledge, and test your dream against God's word. The

---

59   Bruce Wilkinson, *The Dream Giver* (Sisters Publishing: Multnomah, 2003), 150.

principles found in God's love letter to us cover all contingencies, if we know how to interpret them.

A good journaling exercise would be to use a concordance to look up key words associated with your dream to see if there are scriptures related to them. Write out the verses that speak to you. See if you can draw a conclusion about what you've learned after writing and praying about your findings.

Another inquiry is—have we asked enough questions to get the proper answers? We live in such an either/or world. We often stop too soon and don't ask enough questions. *Shall we do this or that?* And then we stop asking, when there is another answer just waiting to be born—a third or fourth option that is better than either of the first two.

When faced with a dilemma, try asking a different question. Jesus seldom directly answered the questions asked of him. Instead he went to the heart of the matter and asked the questions that would meet the need of the questioner—the question or comment that would transform lives.

Doubts and fears, risks and sacrifices are common elements of turning dreams into reality. When you unleash a dream, fear may come right behind it. Recognize the fear for what it is—a self-defense mechanism—then push through it to success, if you know your dream is God-designed.

Once we commit to boldly living out our dreams, we begin to realize how great a need we have to be able to trust in God. We'll learn more about how we can do that in our next chapter.

ACTION STEPS:
Some Practical Advice for Carrying Out Visions

1. Pray, pray, pray, pray. And get others to pray with and for you.

2. Write in a journal, if that helps. Do you suppose David's Psalms were his way of journaling—venting his anger one time, then praising his maker the next?
3. Listen to critics, but with careful discernment.
4. Take action. You don't have to see the whole path from the beginning—sometimes just enough to get you to the next step.
5. Remember: A failed plan (implementation) is not a failed dream (vision).
6. Revise the plan when necessary.

Olympic Dreams

"I don't jump the highest" says Olympic diver, Laura Wilkinson. "I don't spin the fastest. I don't have the best entry. But I'm pretty good at all those things... I know diving is what God made me to do. For some reason, he took someone not the right build for diving and gave me success. I think that's cool—and says a lot about God and how he likes to use unlikely things and people."

When asked about her favorite Olympic experience she tells about the moment just before her last dive at the Sydney Olympics in 2000. "Standing on the platform, I looked out over the audience and the pool and tried to memorize the moment. I realized in that instant I was living my dream."

Camerin Courtney, "TCW Talks to Laura Wilkinson," *Today's Christian Woman* (Sept/Oct 2008).

Chapter Seven
Authentic Trusting: Taking faith steps and trusting God for the future

"Let the morning bring me word of your unfailing love, for I have put my trust in you. Show me the way I should go, for to you I lift up my soul."

Psalm 143:8

> *We are afraid of that which we cannot control, so we continue to draw in the boundaries around us, to limit ourselves to what we can know and understand. Thus we lose our human calling because we do not dare to be creators, co-creators with God.*[60]
>
> **Madeleine L'Engle,** *Walking on Water*

We say we trust God, but do we really? In Chapter Two we talked about hearing God's voice. But what good is hearing if we don't follow and obey? And how can we obey if we don't trust?

---

60   Madeleine L'Engle, *Walking on Water* (Colorado Springs, Colo.: WaterBrook Press, 2001), 191.

It's not that faith and trust are completely foreign concepts to us. Every day we sit in chairs without wondering whether or not they will hold us. We flip light switches, expecting electricity to flow. We trust our words to computers (sometimes with fear and trepidation!) and expect to see them again the next day.

But will we trust our future to God?

In my mind, faith and trust are so intertwined that it's hard to think of one and not the other. We experience faith and trust all the time in ordinary ways. I have faith in you because you have already shown yourself to be trustworthy. Therefore, I will trust you to be honest with me and treat me fairly.

I can say the same for God. In numerous and varied ways, God has already shown himself to be trustworthy, both in my own life and in the life stories of other people I know. I have made a choice to trust God, to put my faith in him. Does this mean I never have any doubts? No. Sometimes I fret and worry and think, *This time it may be different. Maybe God won't be there when I need him.* Then I remember the verse that has sustained me so often, "Fear not, for I have redeemed you…" (Isaiah 43:1b), and I venture out again with tiny faith steps, in the direction I feel God is leading.

That's relatively easy for me to do today, when life is going smoothly. It was not so easy many years ago on the day my doctor told me what he had just discovered during my six-week postpartum check-up.

"There's an ovarian cyst about the size of an orange," he said. "We'll need to operate. It could be benign, but we won't know until we remove it."

In addition to our newborn baby boy we had an 18-month old daughter. I was devastated. I was so afraid I would not live to see my babies grow up. I prayed for healing and tried to trust God for the outcome.

Fortunately, the tumor was benign. We were grateful beyond words, and my anxiety about the future was abated for awhile.

We think we would like to know what the future holds, but God, in his wisdom, keeps that information from us. We are given a choice. We can live in fear of the future or trust that God will take care of us no matter what our future includes.

I appreciate having people pray for me in times of need, and I am privileged to be able to pray for others. Although I don't fully understand how prayer works, I don't believe that a less than positive outcome is a result of too little faith or too few prayers. Yet, we hear people say we just need to have more faith, to trust more, and we can have anything we want.

Larry Osborne, author of *A Contrarian's Guide to Knowing God* has said, "'Faith' today is defined as positive thinking... we're always telling people they need more faith, and most people interpret that as more positive thinking—absolute removal of doubt.

"The real meaning of faith is trust. Trust can have room for doubt and fear...Jesus was saying [in the story about faith as big as a mustard seed], 'No, you need to be more obedient. Quit worrying about your doubts and fears.'"[61]

No matter what the outcome of a diagnosis, a job interview, a troubled teenager's lifestyle, an unhappy marriage, Jesus is telling us we have enough faith if we have *any* faith, that what we need to do is obey and trust God for the outcome, whatever that may be. That is not to say we shouldn't pray for healing

---

[61] "Q&A: Obeying the light you have," *United Methodist Reporter* (September 19, 2008), 7A.

of all kinds in our troubled world, but we can trust God to be present in our lives no matter what the result.

We can trust and cling to the verse that says, "And we know that in all things God works for the good of those who love him, who have been called according to his purpose." Romans 8:28

King Hezekiah's 15 year reprieve
Probably the most defining moment in my husband's life and the lives of his three brothers took place when he was eight years old. His mother had fallen gravely ill and was not expected to recover. However, his father was familiar with the story of King Hezekiah's illness as recorded in 2 Kings, chapter 20, where it says God added 15 years to Hezekiah's life after Hezekiah prayed for healing.

Late one night, Mr. Lee brought his four sons into the master bedroom and positioned them around their mother's bed, lined up from the youngest to the oldest—from three years old to sixteen. Then he prayed, "Lord, I'm asking you to do for Kathryn what you did for King Hezekiah. I'm asking for fifteen more years to be added to her life. You know I can't raise these boys by myself. In fifteen years this youngest boy will be grown and able to make it on his own."

Although in poor health throughout the next fifteen years, and despite being so close to death that funeral arrangements were made three different times, Mrs. Lee saw her youngest son graduate from high school. Not only was she able to help raise her four boys, see two of them marry and enjoy two grandchildren, but she was an inspiration to hundreds of people who saw her valiant struggle and knew of her complete trust in God, in spite of her suffering.

Authentic Trusting: Taking faith steps and trusting God for the future

Fifteen years after that late-night prayer, Kathryn Lee's long struggle ended, but her legacy of faith and trust has been carried on by the sons who surrounded her bed that night.

"You may know what it is to walk in darkness," says pastor and author John Ortberg. "Sometimes faith is walking in darkness and simply refusing to quit. Sometimes faith is just hanging on. The character of the faith that allows us to be transformed by suffering and darkness is not doubt-free certainty; rather, it is tenacious obedience."[62]

Learning to trust God

Can we trust God enough to honestly ask questions about our faith? Do we dare question our belief? Jesus said we must become like little children. A child has absolute faith in her parents, but she also asks a lot of 'why' questions. God understands that we have questions; asking them is for our benefit. A young child asks, "Why, why, why?" then trusts, anyway.

Philip Yancey says, "Prayer allows a place for me to bring my doubts and complaints—in sum, my ignorance—and subject them to the blinding light of a reality I cannot comprehend but can haltingly learn to trust."[63]

For many of us, trust does not come easily. It calls for openness and the ability to lay everything out before God for examination. Instead of covering up our doubts and fears, we are invited to be honest and transparent—to be authentic. We're so accustomed to working to make it look like we have it all

---

[62] John Ortberg, *The Life You've Always Wanted*, (Grand Rapids, Michigan: Zondervan, 2002), 212.

[63] Philip Yancey, *Prayer: Does It Make Any Difference* (Grand Rapids, Michigan: Zondervan, 2006), 40.

together; it's hard for us to admit that we don't have life figured out. We need to practice trusting God for who we can become.

Donald Miller, in his book *Blue Like Jazz,* confesses, "At the end of the day, when I am lying in bed and I know the chances of any of our theology being exactly right are a million to one, I need to know that God has things figured out, that if my math is wrong we are still going to be okay. And wonder is that feeling we get when we let go of our silly answers, our mapped out rules that we want God to follow. I don't think there is any better worship than wonder."[64]

By admitting that we don't have all the answers, we're confessing that we are not God.

Father knows best

Whether we are contemplating trusting God for some momentous change in our lives or simply for daily decision making, prayer is the channel through which we can lay our concerns before the Father who loves us and wants only what is best for us.

Once we understand that God does indeed have our best interest in mind and is trustworthy, our work has just begun. We need to acknowledge that his will is superior to our will. We must choose to walk in the path he has created for us if we hope for peace and fulfillment in our lives.

I've learned so much about innate human behavior from watching my two granddaughters, Abby and Lily. (I was so busy and tired when my own children were toddlers, I missed the important messages!)

---

64 Donald Miller, *Blue Like Jazz* (Nashville, Tennessee: Thomas Nelson, 2003), 206.

We took Abby to a toy store just before Christmas when she was around two years old. Looking back, I realize that's a cruel thing to do to a child. I handed her a toy for entertainment while she rode in the cart as her mother and I shopped. Nevertheless, she continuously reached out to every other toy we passed, with her baby language cries expressing clearly, "I want that thing, too. And that and that!" It was not a pretty sight.

How like toddlers we are as we look around and want everything we see. We're not sure God really has our best in mind. We want to taste all the fruit in the garden.

Lily had her own lessons to teach us. Her mother discovered her one day with a look on her face like the proverbial cat that swallowed the canary. Lily had eaten her sister's peanut butter snack when her mother's back was turned. She knew she had done something forbidden to her. All her body language said so. What she didn't understand at that age was that it is forbidden to her because it's not good for her. She's allergic to peanut butter. Her decision to do something she knew she was not supposed to do resulted in an emergency trip to the doctor's office. Fortunately, her allergic reaction was quickly contained by medication. (And all peanut butter was removed from the house!)

Even as adults we're not much different. As I said in Chapter One, we are all Eve. We look to the forbidden for what we think will bring us pleasure. But God says, "I know the plans I have for you..." Jeremiah 29:11

Can we trust that God's plans for us are really in our best interest? Can we give up our scattered, I-want-it-all approach, for one that focuses on trusting God for what we need in order to live authentically as his child?

Trusting God in the big ideas

"Then I heard the voice of the Lord saying, 'Whom shall I send? And who will go for us?' And I said, 'Here am I. Send me!'" Isaiah 6:8

Notice the exclamation point. Can we answer God's call with such enthusiasm?

Sometimes we have trouble believing God can use us in ways that can make a difference in the world. We must trust that God can and will do a greater work in us than we are capable of on our own.

"The challenge is to let my intellect work *for* the creative act, not against it," says Madeleine L'Engle in *Walking on Water*. "And this means, first of all, that I must have more faith in the work than I have in myself."[65]

We feel God is calling us, but it's hard to trust that we've heard correctly.

When we were preparing to go to China in the 1980's we met barrier after barrier. After a while we wondered if we would ever get there. Friends kept asking us, *Aren't you ever going? Haven't you left yet?* We wished we had not let anyone know about our plans. At one point we were traveling through our home state and came across a city limit sign for China, Texas. We stopped the car and jumped out to take pictures of one another standing under the sign proclaiming "CHINA." Now we could at least say to our friends that we had been to China!

We had felt sure we were supposed to go to the Peoples Republic of China, yet after a year, the whole business venture that was supposed to get us there fell through. It was a perplexing time. Had we misunderstood our calling?

We could not have imagined the answer God had in mind.

---

[65] Madeleine L'Engle, 215.

For several months previously we had been exchanging weekly language and culture sessions with a young businessman from China. We dreaded telling him the distressing news that we would not be going to his country. We greeted Mr. Li with somber faces the next Thursday night and explained what had happened.

He was silent a few seconds, then asked us, "Would you be willing to come teach at my school [his college alma mater] if I can get you an invitation?"

"In a heartbeat! You get us the invitation and we'll be there."

So instead of going with my husband's company to Beijing, as we thought we would, we went as college professors and lived on campus in Anhui Province, experiencing China in a much more intimate way than if we had gone as we first envisioned.

Living in China was not easy, but we never doubted that we were right where we were supposed to be for that time in our lives. Through all the challenges of getting there, we had seen the hand of God orchestrating the plan, and we trusted that he would see us through. We drew on the strength promised us in Philippians 4:13. "I can do everything through him who gives me strength."

We can have faith in the work at hand when we know God has called us to it.

Stepping out in faith

In the Old Testament we read about Joshua leading the children of Israel to claim the land God had promised them. However, there was a predicament. How were all those people supposed to get across The Jordan River?

"Now the Jordan is at flood stage all during harvest. Yet as soon as the priests who carried the ark reached the Jordan and their feet touched the water's edge, the water from upstream stopped flowing...So the people crossed over opposite Jericho. The priests who carried the ark of the covenant of the LORD stood firm on dry ground in the middle of the Jordan, while all Israel passed by until the whole nation had completed the crossing on dry ground." Joshua 3:15-17

When we are unsure of our right path, we want to see the waters part before we step in. But God told Joshua that the priests were to step into the Jordan and *then* the waters would be held back.

John Ortberg tells us, "Taking action is very powerful. The reason many people become paralyzed in discouragement is because they fail to devote the time or energy to understand what was involved in the failure in the first place, and then they fail to take action toward change. They wait for some outside force or person to rescue them when God is calling them to action."[66]

I have several small oil lamps made of clay that came from Israel, replicas of a type of lamp used in Bible times. Each will fit in the palm of my hand. They couldn't have given off much light, I think, because the flame would not be very big. The lamps rest on a bookshelf near my desk as a reminder that I don't have to see the whole path before me; I need just enough light to take the next step.

Trusting God in every season of life

God may be calling us to trust him as we re-define who we are at each stage of our lives. Women today have amazing

---

66   John Ortberg, *If You Want to Walk on Water, You've Got to Get Out of the Boat* (Grand Rapids, Michigan: Zondervan, 2001), 143.

opportunities to make a difference at home and around the world. Never before in our country have so many women been so well educated, so healthy and so wealthy.

So often we spend our time looking forward to the next phase of life instead of appreciating what life brings us now. We wait for the right job, the right husband, for children to be born, for the children to be grown. We can spend our entire lives waiting for the right time to start living.

Young women today have a smorgasbord of opportunities available to them, both in their work world and leisure time activities. Many women are seeing their vacations as more than just a time to get away from work. Instead, they are using these occasions to reach out to people in need in their own communities and around the world. These spirited women are building houses in poor neighborhoods, serving meals to the homeless, tutoring children, advocating for justice for those who don't have a voice, and in many other ways, making their mark on the world.

When we reach middle age (whenever that is) and we're looking at the second half of life, there are more opportunities than ever to re-create ourselves.

If you are wondering what to do with the second half of your life, Dale Hanson Bourke's book, *Second Calling: finding passion & purpose for the rest of your life* may help you see with new eyes.

Ms. Bourke says:

"I love the idea that we have to turn our backs on some of those identities from the first half of life in order to move toward something more authentic in the second. It's not so much that we are losing our identities, but rather that we are no longer embracing false identities. If we hold on to what once defined us, we will miss out on the authentic identity we are being called to."[67]

For some of us, trusting God with direction in life is easier than trusting God with our wrinkles! Can I trust that God can help me see past my aging face to understand that I can do great and mighty things for him, or am I still trying to ignore the fact that I've aged? Can I age gracefully?

Dale Bourke insists that the best is not behind us.

"If we can understand what God is calling us to and can turn away from those voices calling us to stay attached to our youth, we will be given a power and purpose beyond anything we have experienced."[68]

Are we ready to move into our greatness, soaring and becoming all that God has created us to be? Or do we stay stuck on the ground, looking at the wrong role models and lamenting that we are no longer the young women we used to be?

Are we giving up things of real significance for Botox and trading our birthrights, like Esau did, for a biscuit and a bowl of bean soup? Are we more interested in our looks, wealth and status than Godliness?

There's nothing wrong with looking great or having wealth and status. God can and has used many people with those attributes. But if the trappings that we hold dear are not ordained by God for us, we are living diminished lives.

Ms. Bourke says, "If you listen carefully, you will hear a whisper. It is not the cacophony of advertisers telling you to hide your fine lines and wrinkles. It is something far more pervasive and subtle. It is a whisper that says you are being called to something new. It is a gentle voice that seems to say, 'Ah,

---

[67] Dale Hanson Bourke, *Second Calling: finding passion & purpose for the rest of your life* (Brentwood, TN: Integrity Publishers 2006), 122.
[68] Ibid., 8.

now I have your attention.' It is a voice that has been patiently waiting to speak truth you would be able to hear...if you listen hard enough, you hear something holy in that whisper. It is not a voice of doom but of promise. It is not about condemnation but about deliverance. It does not say that you are all washed up but that you are being baptized into a new life."[69]

As we said in the last chapter, there's no retirement plan from God. He wants to use us at any age. We need to concentrate on what we can do, not what we can't.

At our house we keep a list of people who have broken through the age barriers that our culture wants to saddle us with. Motivational and inspirational speakers Zig Ziglar and Florence Littauer are on our list. I consider both of them role-models and mentors. At an age when many people are watching the world go by, these two and others like them are still out there speaking to others of hope and promise. As long as we can be active there is work to be done.

Even when we are unable to participate in some activities, God has a plan for our lives. Have you ever met a mighty prayer warrior? We should all be in a spirit of prayer at all times, but for a committed Christian who is unable to participate in more physical types of activities, holding up others in prayer is something they can do. It's important work and it's available to everyone.

Learning from others

We can benefit from stories in the Bible of godly people who lived before us. I used to think I would like to have lived in 1st century Jerusalem. It would have been easier to believe, I thought. But would it have been? I'm a natural skeptic.

---

69   Ibid., 2-3.

I might have seen Jesus and thought up dozens of reasons why I shouldn't follow him. But by living now we have the witness of Godly people down through the centuries. Ours is not a blind trust but a trust partially based on lives that have gone before us.

Don't you love the so-called "Roll call of the saints" in Hebrews 11? "By faith Enoch...By faith Noah...By faith Abraham..." on and on it goes. It's as if God wanted to leave a record of the faith of the ancients so those who would come afterwards could understand that they are not the first to step out on faith.

The Hebrews 11 account of courageous faith is not of people who were sinless. Rahab, Samson, David, Moses and others listed were people who had committed what we consider major sins but who also committed themselves to be used by God.

It's fascinating to see how God brings events together for His purposes and the world's good. Even though we feel inadequate to do God's work, he chooses to use flawed vessels. *We are chosen.*

Do you remember the Old Testament story of Ruth and Naomi? What an unlikely person Ruth was to be the ancestor of Jewish kings and even the Messiah. She was not one of the chosen people, as the Israelites knew themselves to be. Yet because of her faithfulness to her mother-in-law Naomi, and embracing Naomi's God, God used Ruth in spite of her inadequacies.

We dwell on our past mistakes instead of accepting God's forgiveness and grace. Instead of embracing who we are in Christ, we keep re-visiting our past and telling God why we aren't qualified to do kingdom work.

Authentic Trusting: Taking faith steps and trusting God for the future

God is all about present and future, not past. The things we need to remember from the past are times and ways that God brought us through hardships. We need to learn from our past but not dwell there.

I'm eager for our journey to continue. We can take the next step by planning our lives, depending on God's leading and taking the initiative to live intentionally.

ACTION STEPS:
Writing About Your Faith Walk

1. Create a timeline of your life, separated into increments of five or ten years.
2. Write about your earliest memories concerning God. Were you a child in church singing next to your parents? Or perhaps you had little contact with spiritual experiences until adulthood.
3. How did you come to a decision to follow Christ? Who was

> **Remembering Our Faith Journey**
>
> Like the Israelites wandering in the desert, we don't learn our lessons easily. God cautioned them to remember the provisions he had supplied in the past. We need to do the same.
>
> By writing about how God has preserved or rescued us, these experiences can reinforce our trust.
>
> In Joshua 4:5-7 we read, "[Joshua] said to them, 'Go over before the ark of the LORD your God into the middle of the Jordan. Each of you is to take up a stone on his shoulder, according to the number of the tribes of the

instrumental in this event? Where were you? How old were you? What else was going on in your life at the time.
4. Brainstorm about times God has worked in your life—maybe difficult or exciting changes, illnesses, difficulties with other people, job loss, etc. Make note of the good times and the bad.
5. If you would like, put your experiences into a written journal or scrapbook, adding pictures and illustrations.
6. Share with friends and family and pass it on to those who come after you.

> Israelites, to serve as a sign among you. In the future, when your children ask you, 'What do these stones mean?' tell them that the flow of the Jordan was cut off before the ark of the covenant of the LORD. When it crossed the Jordan, the waters of the Jordan were cut off. These stones are to be a memorial to the people of Israel forever.'"
>
> We can leave a record of God's faithfulness that not only will remind us to trust when things get tough, but it also leaves a legacy to our descendants to help them along their faith journeys.

Chapter Eight
Authentic Planning: Embracing the courage to change step by step

"Show me your ways, O Lord, teach me your paths; guide me in your truth and teach me, for you are God my Savior, and my hope is in you all day long."

Psalm 25:4-5

> *As Christians we serve a mighty God, the creator of the universe, a God who is bigger than we can possibly imagine. It is that mighty God who has created our divine destiny, a destiny that is also bigger than we can imagine. Where our life pictures are rooted in common sense, the mighty God we serve has created a purpose for our lives that almost always defies common sense.*[70]
>
> **Kimberly Dunnam Reisman,** *Knowing God*

We have seen that we can trust God to show us how to live in ways that would fulfill us and bless others. Now we have a

---

[70] Kimberly Dunnam Reisman, *Knowing God: Making God the Main Thing in My Life* (Nashville, TN: Abingdon Press, 2003), 145.

responsibility to examine our lives and align our thoughts with God's best plan.

As we make plans to carry out our dreams, we pray with the Psalmist: "Show me your ways, O LORD, teach me your paths..."

Seeking God's will

Sometimes we pray and pray for God to show us his will when the answer is right in front of us. We overlook the very practical ways of finding an answer, waiting for a supernatural word.

When I was considering quitting my day job to write full time, I had one of my silent dialogues with God.

"Lord, if I just had some kind of sign that writing is what I should be doing," I whined.

The thought immediately came to me, as if it were a word from God: *What kind of sign would you need to make you feel this is the right thing to do?*

I started to answer, "If I just had a publisher's contract, something that confirmed..." Before I got the thoughts fully formed, I realized how ridiculous that suggestion must seem to God. I already had a contract for writing children's Sunday school curriculum. How had I overlooked that fact? I guess I was thinking I would feel affirmed if I had a book contract. I totally dismissed what I already had because it was different from what I expected. I felt like Gideon and his fleece. I wasn't satisfied with the first sign; I wanted another one.

I'm glad God doesn't reject me when I'm so dense!

I needed to follow the advice Paul gave to the Romans: "Do not conform any longer to the pattern of this world, but be transformed by the renewing of your mind. Then you will be able to test and approve what God's will is—his good, pleasing and perfect will." Romans 12:2

Another mistake we make is not seeking God's input first. Instead of asking what God has in mind for us, then aligning our ideas with his, we sometimes make our own plans then ask God to bless them. Unfortunately, I've frequently implemented my own plans until I get to a point that I can't make things happen my way. Then I ask God to step in and make something good out of my mess. How much better it would be if I would seek God's guidance from the beginning.

Embracing Change
If I am to boldly follow God's divine purposes for my life, I must be willing to make the changes that will allow me to soar. Understanding how change works helps me move through the adjustments I need to make.

According to *The Change Cycle*, by Ann Salerno and Lillie Brock, how we cope with change will be determined by how well we adapt—emotionally, mentally, spiritually and physically. They define six predictable stages we go through when faced with change: loss, doubt, discomfort, discovery, understanding and integration.

Stage 1, Loss, is characterized by feelings of fear and a sense of loss of what existed before. Stage 2, Doubt, brings resentment and resistance. Stage 3, Discomfort, results in anxiety and confusion. Stage 4, Discovery, may bring anticipation and creativity. Stage 5, Understanding, moves us to feel confident and we become productive. The final stage, Stage 6, Integration, allows us to focus our thoughts, regain ability and be willing to be flexible.

Salerno and Brock say "The Danger Zone" comes after Stage 3, when we decide to either move on to Stage 4, discovering the possibilities the change brings and moving on, or go back to Stage 1 and be fearful of the change.

"For all we know about the science and predictability of change, there is still the mystery of intensity when it comes to individual reactions," they say. "A change that might rock one person's world can be a speed bump to another. Each of us experiences change with our own scoreboard correlating to where we are on our path through life."[71]

An important part of maturation is to realize that change is inevitable. We need to learn to grow with the changes that come our way. Understanding that we likely will go through a change cycle before we can move on, helps us to be more patient with ourselves and others as they try to change. In order to follow God's exciting plan for our lives, we must be ready to change and become more than we thought possible, to shed our cocoon and unfurl our wings. We don't want to be making plans for the person we used to be, when God is calling us to become new creations.

Creating a purpose statement

Many people find it helpful to have a personal mission, purpose, or vision statement. Businesses have been doing this for years, but it's not so common in personal life. Having a well thought out statement can help us make decisions about how we should spend our time, energy and money. The terms "mission statement," "purpose statement" and "vision statement" have been used interchangeably sometimes and have been

---

71 Ann Salerno and Lillie Brock, *The Change Cycle* (San Francisco: Barrett-Koehler Publishers, Inc., 2008), 5.

defined in different ways by different people. For our use, I'll just call it a Purpose Statement and define it as a statement that will guide our decisions about how to live our lives. (At the end of this chapter we will look at some specifics for creating such a statement.)

Having a well thought out Purpose Statement may or may not result in our choosing a new profession, but it can provide an over-arching statement of who we feel called to be. It can keep us focused on the important things and help us escape from living frenetic lives, chasing after every "bright, shiny object" that comes across our path.

As we saw in Chapter One, we have so many choices we can become paralyzed when trying to figure out what we should be doing. If we are not intentional about how we live, we will bounce around, reacting to life as it hits us. By concentrating on who we are and what we are called to do, we can begin to focus on what we do best and work in our strengths.

Once we've discovered who we were created to be (even though we may not have been living it out fully), we can say 'no' to the things that no longer fit our purpose. Certainly, we will sometimes need to go outside this ideal to meet truly important needs such as caring for sick family members, responding to crises, or other true emergencies. But it's important for us to be able to recognize the difference between urgent and important matters—especially those things that are urgent only to someone else. You've probably seen the sign, "Failure to plan on your part does not constitute an emergency on my part." We need to learn how to say something like this, kindly but firmly, to those people who would be glad to use our time in ways that only benefit them!

I remember a Bible teacher talking to a group of parents about how to use our time effectively. One young woman complained that there just wasn't enough time to do everything she had to do. The teacher began questioning her about her activities and suggested that she let go of at least one of the responsibilities she had taken on.

"But if I don't do it, no one else will." It was more of a wail than a statement.

"Let me see if I understand what you've told us," the wise teacher said. "There are over 100 people in the organization, and you are the *only* one who will take on this task?"

"That's right!"

"If out of more than 100 people, you are the only one who will volunteer to do this," he asked quietly and kindly, "how badly does the job need to be done?"

Silence reigned.

I don't know about the others, but I began doing an inventory of all the spinning plates I had up in the air and wondered how many of them I could let go of. It occurred to me that some of the activities I had agreed to do made me feel important or needed, even though they weren't adding substance to my life.

How to turn a dream into reality?

I encourage my coaching clients not to worry about the *how* until they know the *what* and *why*. If we don't know what we want in life and why we want it, it's impossible to map out a meaningful path. Even when we understand our real passion and why it matters to us, we can still get hung up. We think we couldn't possibly accomplish our heart's desire because we don't know how, it would cost too much, or it would take too much time.

But God has a plan in mind and we can trust him to guide us if we let him. Through prayer, listening (as we learned in

Chapter Two) and following God's nudging, we can begin to see a pathway.

Once we are clear on the direction we want to go in life, our creativity steps in to show us ways of getting there. Our minds open up to possibilities we never noticed before. People who hold pieces to the puzzle come into our lives.

Persistence and perseverance—

We get discouraged sometimes when things don't happen right away. We give up too soon. We fear failure so much that if our dream doesn't come easily, we decide it's not worth pursuing. We think we have misunderstood our calling, and we get frustrated and ready to give up, when it may be that the timing is not right. When this happens, it's good to remember our past successes, especially those that did not come easily but were accomplished after persevering.

James admonished the early Christians to "Consider it pure joy, my brothers, whenever you face trials of many kinds, because you know that the testing of your faith develops perseverance. Perseverance must finish its work so that you may be mature and complete, not lacking anything." James 1:2-4

When we face trials, it's time to remember how God led us through past wildernesses. This is when we can get out our "Faith Walk" journal entries, as mentioned at the end of the last chapter. Seeing how God has provided for us in the past gives us strength for the present leg of the journey.

Best laid plans

There are times when in spite of all our careful praying and planning, things do not turn out as we expect. We may even think God is not going to answer our prayers this time when we ask for guidance.

My humorous friend, Betty, has been through many difficult periods in her life. She told me, "At first I prayed, asking God what he wanted me to do. Then I got so frustrated, I would go outside at night, look up at the stars and say, 'Lord, I don't know how to deal with this; could we just leave this problem and go on to the next one?' Now I just go directly to the back door, open it and yell—'Next!'"

Yes, sometimes life throws us curves, even tragedies. Don't waste your pain. You can help others deal with their difficulties through sharing your own situation. Pray for God to reveal how you can best use your experiences, heartaches, abilities, gifts and interests.

Gail Showalter was a single mother of three for 16 years before re-marrying. Her heart beats today with those single women who are raising their children alone. Out of her experiences and pain, Gail has created SMORE: Single Moms - Overjoyed, Rejuvenated, Empowered!

Through retreats and speaking, Gail inspires and encourages single moms to achieve their potential.

"Though I've been happily remarried since 1996 and my three children are grown, I still have a heavy heart for mothers raising children alone. I endured many disappointments during my sixteen years as a single mother. Through it all I learned that every true spiritual experience I've had came out of pain, either mine or that of someone I loved.

"SMORE for Women developed because of my desire to give single moms a break and a blessing. I knew how much it meant when others demonstrated kindness to me during my own tough times. Now it's my turn."[72]

Wherever you are—at home, in business, in community activities, at church activities—you can be a blessing to those around you who are dealing with dilemmas you've already been through.

I could never do that!

Above my computer screen I have posted a note that says, "No obstacles; just opportunities! Take the next logical step."

Obstacles are not the problem. How we face them can be.

It's so easy to be fearful of making a wrong move. Yet if we become immobilized by our fear or uncertainty, we close off the path completely. By not taking a *first* step we keep ourselves from seeing the *next* step.

You don't have to see the end of the path to take the appropriate beginning steps. It's like walking at night with one of those clay lamps from Israel or like taking a walk with a small flashlight. You don't need to see the whole path to its end; you just need to see far enough to take the next step.

And it's okay to take baby steps at first!

Who, me, Lord?

Are you afraid you can't be the person God is calling you to be? Do you hesitate to take any step at all because you think you couldn't possibly succeed? Or maybe you feel it's immodest to think God could use you in the way you would like.

---

[72] Gail Showalter, personal correspondence with the author.

Joyce Meyer in her book *How to Succeed at Being Yourself*, says, "Most of the things that are truly worth doing are never easy—we are not filled with the Spirit of God to do easy things. He fills us with His Spirit so we can do impossible things!"[73]

If you are a child of God and have given your life to him, you are not alone in your journey. You do not have to live in your own strength. God has provided a helper and guide so that you can step up to become the person you were created to be—a person meant to do great things, even impossible things.

Ready to launch

You may not feel ready to live a life of significance. However, if God has led you to do something beyond your comfort zone and beyond your own abilities, he will also equip you and provide the means for you to do it.

Earlier we looked at what it means to be "because you say so" people. We need to be ready to launch out into the deep when Jesus calls us to do so. Let's look at the scriptures and see what the result was for Jesus' followers.

"[Jesus] got into one of the boats, the one belonging to Simon, and asked him to put out a little from shore. Then he sat down and taught the people from the boat.

"When he had finished speaking, he said to Simon, 'Put out into deep water, and let down the nets for a catch.'

"Simon answered, 'Master, we've worked hard all night and haven't caught anything. *But because you say so*, I will let down the nets.' [Italics added.]

---

73   Joyce Meyer, *How to Succeed at Being Yourself* (Fenton, Missouri: Warner Books Edition, 1999), 82.

"When they had done so, they caught such a large number of fish that their nets began to break. So they signaled their partners in the other boat to come and help them, and they came and filled both boats so full that they began to sink.

"When Simon Peter saw this, he fell at Jesus' knees and said, 'Go away from me, Lord; I am a sinful man!' For he and all his companions were astonished at the catch of fish they had taken, and so were James and John, the sons of Zebedee, Simon's partners.

"Then Jesus said to Simon, 'Don't be afraid; from now on you will catch men.' So they pulled their boats up on shore, left everything and followed him." Luke 5:3-11

Those fishermen experienced firsthand what it was like to follow the plan Jesus had in mind. When they realized the Power in the boat with them, it changed their lives. Indeed, they left their old way of living—and making a living—to follow Jesus.

A similar kind of transformation awaits us when we align our lives with the source of all power. Not only will we be transformed, but we can lead others to experience that same power.

We can live in such a way that we reflect the glory of God and can lead others to more fulfilling lives. Let's find out how in the next chapter.

ACTION STEPS:
When working with my coaching clients on creating their mission, ministry, vision and/or purpose statements we discuss some of the following ideas to help them listen to their own lives and carve out their focus. These same ideas may help you discover your authentic self.

Creating a Purpose Statement: A Practical Approach to Living Your Best Life.

1. Pray for God to guide you.
2. In each area of your life, write down what your ideal life would look like. Some areas to include are as follows: Spiritual, Family, Friends, Personal Growth, Work/Business, Financial, Physical, Community (local and worldwide).
3. Where do you find commonalities among all these areas of life? For instance, if you say in several areas, "I want to be a better listener," or "I want to actively participate…" Maybe you want to lead women's groups to learn more about God's word, or you may want to work to help children become healthier. Finding commonalities will give you a clue to what could give more meaning to your life.
4. See if a concise purpose statement can be created from these common denominators. An example might be: "Through speaking, writing and coaching, I will encourage, inspire and motivate women to step into their greatness."

    Then when opportunities come along you can measure them against your statement to see if they fit your plan.

    Even a simple statement like the following can help keep you on track: "Making a difference in the world one small decision at a time, one relationship after another." When faced with a decision, you can ask yourself, *Will this make a positive difference in the world? Is this fostering a relationship?*
5. Does your statement truly resonate with your heart and mind? Remember, this is not a list of "shoulds" but a reflection of who you truly are at your core.
7. Try it out for awhile. Test decisions against it. See if you can say 'no' to things outside of your Purpose Statement.

Authentic Planning: Embracing the courage to change step by step

8. Write your Purpose Statement on a card and post it prominently or keep it near you in your purse or pocket.
9. Read your statement daily and tweak it until it is refined, then internalized.
10. Continue to pray for God to show you where any changes need to be made.

Chapter Nine
Authentic Living: Experiencing life according to God's plan

"They shall again live beneath my shadow, they shall flourish as a garden."

Hosea 14:7a (NRSV)

I have lived in four states in the United States and two countries outside of the U.S. Each place has taught me its own life lessons.

Living in the high desert of New Mexico, as we do now, I've learned to appreciate shade as I never had before. The temperature in the shade is several degrees cooler than just a few inches away in the intense desert sunshine. Gardening here has been a challenge for me. I plant flowers, water them and talk to them, encouraging them to grow. They wither and die. I have learned that when the planting directions say, "Grow in full sun," I have to modify that. Our Southwestern sun is *too* full. Whether the label says so or not, a little shade is called for. Shade comforts and shields the plants, allowing them to put down roots and grow.

In order for us to grow and become who we were created to be, we must lean in so close to God that we are in his shadow. The verse from Hosea at the beginning of this chapter reminds us that no matter what has happened in our past, we can return to God and live in his shadow, protected from the elements that would harm us. Imagine living—flourishing—in the very shadow of the almighty God.

Although I'm not a very talented gardener, I am an eternal optimist. I continue to plant seeds and occasionally, against all odds, they actually grow and bloom.

I looked out my breakfast room window a few months ago and was surprised to see that morning glories were blooming. I had tucked the seeds into the ground just a few weeks earlier thinking I had waited too late, as summer was almost over. But there they were climbing high and rewarding me with large blue and white blossoms turning to magenta as they withered. Then I noticed the vines had grown beyond the top of the ornamental garden stakes I had provided for them, falling back toward the earth in a jumble.

Sometimes I am like those morning glory vines. I get inspired to reach for a goal only to find that I've wrapped myself around the wrong support. It's not high enough. Instead of soaring and attaining my goal, I give up too soon. Or I don't look beyond my present "stake" for something, or Someone, to help me reach even higher.

We want to grow and go farther in life, but we can't see how it could ever come about. We are limited by our human eyes in what we can see happening for us in the future. However, we are called to live boldly, to live "out loud," to leap out of our comfort zones and become women who make a difference in our world.

We need to believe 2 Timothy 1:7—"For God did not give us a spirit of timidity, but a spirit of power, of love and of self-discipline."

Wow! Power, love and self-discipline. What would our lives be like if we took this to heart? Power, instead of fear. Love, instead of fear. Self-discipline, instead of fear. For isn't it fear that makes us timid, holding us back from living the fulfilled, abundant life God calls us to live?

Facing your fears

We have talked about fear before, but it bears repeating. Fear of failure; fear of success; fear of the unknown; fear of inadequacy; fear of rejection; fear of what others will think, fear of embarrassment. The list seems endless. But we don't have to give in to these fears that are of our own making. We can choose to embrace the abundant life Jesus promised to his followers in John 10:10b. "I have come that they may have life, and have it to the full."

We can move from leading lives of quiet desperation, as Henry David Thoreau suggested most people do, to leading lives of quiet contemplation or lives of exuberant celebration! We have a choice. We can live on our own limited terms or choose to live as God intended. If we choose the latter, that will involve growing and changing.

When gardening, not only do I enjoy planting in the ground, but I also like container gardening. It takes a whole different skill-set to garden in containers. In addition to watering regularly and placing the pot where it will receive the appropriate light, I must be sure the size of the container is appropriate to the size of the plant. As the roots grow, if they run out of room to stretch, they will start encircling the inside of the pot. When this happens, the plant has grown too large for the pot and its growth will be stunted.

Like a pot-bound plant, we eventually become unhealthy if we remain in too small a space for the person we are called to become.

Choosing to grow

We are bombarded with so many choices it's easy to get overwhelmed. It takes a conscious decision to choose wisely. Often we must let go of the good to embrace the best.

Several women in the Bible give us examples of how to choose what is best, even in difficult circumstances.

The beloved story of Esther (Hadassah) has encouraged women for centuries to step forward "for such a time as this." Because of her unique position as a Jew in the harem of the Persian King Xerxes, she was able to thwart an attempt to annihilate the Jews living in that country.

Esther's cousin Mordecai learned of the plot against the Jews and implored her to go before the king to plead their case. He told her, "...who knows but that you have come to royal position for such a time as this?" Esther 4:14b

Esther knew that appearing before the king without his specific request to see her was punishable by death. In spite of her great fear, she responded to Mordecai with courage: "Go, gather together all the Jews who are in Susa, and fast for me," she told Mordecai. "Do not eat or drink for three days, night or day. I and my maids will fast as you do. When this is done, I will go to the king, even though it is against the law. And if I perish, I perish." Esther 4:16

Because of Esther's boldness, the Jews in Persia were saved. She is an inspiration to all of us to do what is right regardless of the consequences.

In the New Testament we find a few verses mentioning a woman named Joanna. I became interested in her when I started doing interpretive storytelling of Bible characters. Luke introduces us to her as one of those who took care of Jesus, saying: "Joanna the wife of Cuza, the manager of Herod's household; Susanna; and many others. These women were helping to support them out of their own means." Luke 8:3

Joanna was also one of the women who went to Jesus' tomb and finding it empty told the apostles what they had seen. (Luke 24:10)

So many times we think of Jesus' disciples as only poor male fishermen, yet here was a follower who was the wife of an official in the king's court. When I portray Joanna I usually wear gold jewelry with purple and aqua fabric draped over my head, dressing to signify her high standing as I imagine it (though admittedly taking a rather fanciful approach). It reminds me that whoever I am and whatever I have—whether little or much—I can be used to further God's kingdom.

Another interesting New Testament woman is Lydia, perhaps the first European to accept the gospel. Paul traveled as a missionary to Macedonia and encountered her and a group of women worshippers. I wish I knew more about her. What did her house look like? What did she do for fun? I know she worked with my favorite color, purple. Purple dye was very expensive, reserved for the elite in society, so that gives me a glimpse of her life.

Paul describes meeting Lydia: "On the Sabbath we went outside the city gate to the river, where we expected to find a place of prayer. We sat down and began to speak to the women who had gathered there. One of those listening was a woman named Lydia, a dealer in purple cloth from the city of Thyatira, who was a worshiper of God. The Lord opened her heart to respond to Paul's message. When she and the members of her household were baptized, she invited us to her home. 'If you consider me a believer in the Lord,' she said, 'come and stay at my house.' And she persuaded us." Acts 16:13-15

Lydia eagerly opened her home, showing hospitality to those who had brought God's message of salvation to her and her household.

Each of these biblical women used what they had and were used by God. We are called to live according to God's plan, just as they were.

Distractions from abundant living

There are many things that keep us from living the fulfilling lives to which we have been called.

Perfectionism—

We need to work towards excellence but not be weighed down by perfectionism. Excellence is invigorating; perfectionism is debilitating. However, giving up perfection for excellence is difficult for many women.

I remember as a young wife and mother when I first realized I would never have everything perfect—house, yard, personal appearance. You'd think I would have been relieved. I wasn't. Instead, I was gloomy for weeks. It took some adjustment to give up that hope of perfection.

Now, with the wisdom (or mellowness) that comes with age, I can relax and appreciate life without seeking perfection. I can claim God's competence and give up my own incompetence, agreeing with Paul:

"Not that we are competent in ourselves to claim anything for ourselves, but our competence comes from God." (2 Cor. 3:5)

Those nagging little annoyances—

I suspect that our lives are diminished by little things as often as big ones. What are some of the stress points or energy zappers that irritate you, keeping you from living abundantly?

Often we tolerate things that we don't even notice anymore but that tend to bring us down or hold us back.

They may be little things we do or fail to do, unmet challenges in our relationships or even problems in our physical environment. From time to time we need to take inventory of our surroundings, our relationships and our habits to see if we are living intentionally or if we've fallen into the trap of taking things as they come and putting up with less than our best. When we become aware of those little annoyances, we can make the decision to remove them from our lives.

Lack of focus—

Another thing that distracts us from the abundant life is not maintaining focus on the goal.

When we fail to examine our lives and have not found that which gives meaning, we will be blown by every wind that catches our attention. At the end of each day we will wonder where the time went and if the hours really counted for anything.

On the other hand, living on purpose and following a God-given path to reach our goals gives meaning and energy to our days.

Lack of balance—

When our lives are out of balance we cannot be all we were created to be. What does balance look like in today's world? While we probably can't spend an equal amount of time daily in each area of our lives—spiritual, physical, mental, emotional, relational—over a period of time we should give attention to each of these. At a given time one area may absorb more of our time and attention than any of the others, such as our children when they are young, but overall we need to spend the appropriate time on each part of our lives so we can experience stability.

Living out your values

Often we are advised to try to live out our core values. It seems like we would do that naturally. However, if we continually fail to live according to our perceived values, maybe our true values are not what we would like them to be.

The apostle Paul understood this and said, "I do not understand what I do. For what I want to do I do not do, but what I hate I do. And if I do what I do not want to do, I agree that the law is good. As it is, it is no longer I myself who do it, but it is sin living in me." Romans 7:15-17

Let's look at some areas important in living an authentic life.

Integrity

An authentic woman is one who can be trusted at all times. If our word is not good for the small things we encounter, we will not be trusted in the larger ones.

Dignity

Living our own lives with dignity and treating all other people with that same dignity adds a measure of fullness to our existence. When we allow others to treat us as less than who we are, and when we treat others as less than God's glorious creations, we are reduced in our own estimations.

Perseverance

As we mentioned in the last chapter, we need to persevere when we know what God has called us to do. We may be tempted to give up. If we do, we lose confidence in ourselves and our cause.

Hebrews 10:35-36 says, "So do not throw away your confidence; it will be richly rewarded. You need to persevere so that when you have done the will of God, you will receive what he has promised."

When things don't go as we had planned

Living in the desert has given us lots of metaphors for life. Shortly after moving to New Mexico we returned to the forests of Atlanta to teach our former Sunday school class one Sunday. We called our message, "Lessons Learned in the Desert," and made the following points:

1. Keep Looking Up—it's very brown at ground level in much of our state, but the azure sky makes up for it. If I remember to look up for my sustenance, I am renewed.

2. Get Your Bearings From What Is Constant. Because the Sandia Mountains can be seen from anywhere in the city, we can keep our bearings by looking to that which is not going to change.

3. When Things Look Dark, Don't Despair—Better Times Are Coming. I love to watch the storm clouds rolling in. There will be rain falling over part of the city, while clear blue skies cover the other part. I remember then that what is happening in my life right now is not going to last forever.

As I write this today it is raining, even though most of the sky is intensely blue with only a few scattered clouds. Seemingly out of nowhere, the raindrops fall straight down like shards of glass, reflecting the afternoon sun. The glistening rain reminds me that we can reflect the Son's rays, even during the rainy days of our lives. Much as we would like to avoid them, difficult days teach us things we could never learn in easier times. We can then use our experiences to help others.

Sacred and secular living

We insist on separating life into "sacred" and "secular," when in actuality all of life is sacred. We dare not compartmentalize God, bringing him out on Sundays then shutting him out of our lives for the rest of the week. I recently heard someone scold a friend saying, "You shouldn't curse on Sunday!" I guess he thought God doesn't listen in on our conversations during the rest of the week.

Under the heading, "There is Divine Potential in All You Envision to Do," Andy Stanley reminds us that God is interested in all facets of our lives. "He has positioned you in your culture as a singular point of light. A beacon in a world that desperately needs to see something divine…The truth is, our secular pursuits have more kingdom potential than our religious ones. For it is in the realm of our secular pursuits that secular people are watching."[74]

This is such an important concept. We fear that if we give ourselves to God, we will need to change our vocation, fly to the other side of the world and take a vow of poverty.

---

74 Andy Stanley, *Visioneering* (Sisters, Oregon: Multnomah Publishers, Inc., 1999), 225.

Instead, God may want to use you right where you are. A committed believer living out God's truths in the workplace has the potential of reaching as many hurting people with Good News as does a preacher in the pulpit.

Being vs. doing

We've talked a lot in these chapters about what we should do. Indeed, there are times when we are called to do mighty things. However, we are in danger of always judging ourselves and others by what we have accomplished, when God may just want us to *be* for a while—to hear the next word from him.

There comes a time to stop planting, watering and weeding the garden and simply enjoy the color and fragrance of the flowers. We need to be still and listen for the voice of God, soaking up his love for us.

Madeleine L'Engel understands this. She says, "And then there is time in which to be, simply to be, that time in which God quietly tells us who we are and who he wants us to be. It is then that God can take our emptiness and fill it up with what he wants and drain away the business with which we inevitably get involved in the dailiness of human living."[75]

Living with authentic success

When I started my coaching and speaking business I thought of a variety of different names, then settled on Authentic Success. Who doesn't want to feel successful in life? Yet, there's so much more to true success than just making a ton of money or gaining prestige. Some of the wealthiest, most recognized people

---

75   Madeleine L'Engle, *Walking on Water* (Colorado Springs, Colo.: Water-Brook Press, 2001), 203.

in America have proven this over and over. Sports, Hollywood and Wall Street figures have become clichés for messed up lives.

In the gospel of Mark we read: "What good is it for a man to gain the whole world, yet forfeit his soul? Or what can a man give in exchange for his soul?" Mark 8:36-37

If we are living only for our own success in our business or personal life, we risk missing the most important gifts awaiting us.

An authentic life is an integrated life. We cannot separate spiritual and secular life, nor core values and business practices, if we wish to live according to God's plan. Instead, we can look for the holy in all aspects of life. We can create businesses that uphold and proclaim the worth of all people. In our communities we can model behavior that reflects a message of hope. In our families we can create havens of peace and support.

When we have learned to live as we were created to live, depending on God's power, not our own, we will indeed flourish like a garden in the shadow of the Almighty God.

There is more to life than acquiring goods and seeking acclaim. Are you ready to lead others to discover how to become authentic? Without preaching or pushing our beliefs on others, we can lead by living out the gospel message. We'll look at how to do that in our last chapter.

ACTION STEPS:
Understanding Your Vision to Live an Authentic Life

Spend some time looking at your answers to the following questions, then write a description of your *ideal* life, incorporating the things most important to you.

Authentic Living: Experiencing life according to God's plan

1. Do you have favorite verses in the Bible? If so, write them down and meditate on them. If you haven't discovered favorite verses, be open to what you read and hear in sermons and make note of the ones that stand out.
2. What activities do you most enjoy doing?
3. What words come to mind when you think about the kinds of things you like to be involved in? List them quickly—nouns, adjectives, whatever comes to mind.
4. What do you think about at night before falling asleep?
5. When do you feel the most like yourself? Most complete?
6. Whom do you admire most? Why?
7. In what areas have you felt successful in the past?
8. What would you like to contribute to the world? To your community? To your church?

Addressing energy zappers that hold you back—

1. Take inventory of your life and write down what activities, circumstances and people add energy and joy and which ones deplete your energy and joy. These may be large or small challenges.
2. Ask God to show you how to solve the challenges.
3. State the negatives as positive, solvable solutions. i.e. Kitchen cabinets need painting. I'll call and get several estimates by Jan. 30.

9. What are 10 things you value in life? Of those, which five are the most important to you?
10. If you think "really big," what could you see yourself doing? What is holding you back from doing it?

(This doesn't solve the whole problem but is a step in identifying the solution.)

4. Make a list of the steps needed to solve the challenge. Do step 1, then keep stepping!

5. Stay focused on the problem until it's taken care of. (Don't try to take on too many challenges at once. Prioritize your list and choose to tackle one to three items at a time.)

Chapter Ten
Authentic Leading: Becoming a beacon to those around you

"NO ONE LIGHTS A LAMP AND hides it in a jar or puts it under a bed. Instead, he puts it on a stand, so that those who come in can see the light."

Luke 8:16

> *There are people who need what you have—weak people who need your strength, blind people who need your insight, captives who need to be set free.*[76]
>
> **Stephen Arterburn,** *Flashpoints*

In our time together we've learned to ask questions and to listen for the answers, to stand tall and realize our worth in God's eyes, to forgive and be forgiven. We've grown in many ways, embraced our dreams, trusted God to use us, made plans for the future and are now beginning to live out those plans. We've covered a lot of territory, but our work is not done.

---

76   Stephen Arterburn, *Flashpoints* (Wheaton, Illinois: Tyndale House, 2002), 142.

Following God's call is essential not only for our own good but for those people around us who are looking for direction. You can be a steady beacon shining in an uncertain world.

Whether or not you know who it is, there is someone looking at your life, hoping to find answers for their own. You don't need a theology or counseling degree in order to help someone who is not quite as far along in their journey as you are.

The world is looking for leaders. Many of us want to learn how to be our best in all aspects of life. According to the January 2009 issue of *Success* magazine, the field of personal and professional development has become a $10 billion industry. Seminars, self-help books and various forms of media make it possible to learn almost anything we need to know, and we are eager to learn from those who we think have answers to our success in life. Sometimes we follow leaders without even knowing what their credentials are. We're hungry for someone to tell us how to be more than we are.

Where do you fit into the puzzle of how to help others become the persons they were created to be? What expertise do you possess that can benefit others? What qualifies you to be a leader? You are qualified because you are called by God to use your abilities and experiences to help others.

Called to lead

Kim Reisman encourages us, saying, "Jesus calls us to full discipleship, not a partial façade of discipleship that makes exceptions for us because we are women. Our sense of balance and wholeness is heightened when we listen to the voice of God, calling us in directions uniquely suited to our gifts and talents."[77]

---

77 Kimberly Dunnam Reisman, *The Christ Centered Woman: Finding Balance in a World of Extremes* (Nashville, Tennessee: Upper Room Books, 2000), 85.

Reluctant leaders

If you feel reluctant to lead, join the band of Biblical leaders who hesitated before answering God's call, resisted change or just didn't feel adequate to the task:

Moses—Moses protested when God called him to lead his people out of Egypt, "What if they do not believe me or listen to me and say, 'The LORD did not appear to you'?" Exodus 4:1

Yet in spite of his hesitation, Moses eventually faced the Egyptian Pharaoh and went on to lead the Israelites out of slavery.

Gideon—"But Lord," Gideon asked, "how can I save Israel? My clan is the weakest in Manasseh, and I am the least in my family." Judges 6:15

Even "the least" was able to lead an army of Israelites to defeat the Midianites, as part of God's plan of creating a nation that would honor the one, true God.

Elijah—"There he went into a cave and spent the night. And the word of the LORD came to him: 'What are you doing here, Elijah?' He replied, 'I have been very zealous for the LORD God Almighty. The Israelites have rejected your covenant, broken down your altars, and put your prophets to death with the sword. I am the only one left, and now they are trying to kill me too.'" 1 Kings 19:9-10

Even though Elijah was running scared, fearful for his life and seemed to have a "poor me" attitude, he also was used of God in mighty ways.

Remember, we can claim God's promise as Joshua did when God told him: "Have I not commanded you? Be strong and courageous. Do not be terrified; do not be discouraged, for the LORD your God will be with you wherever you go." Joshua 1:9

Decide to take the leap.

Ordinary women used by God bring extraordinary results

We don't feel adequate to our calling to become leaders because we don't understand the plan God has in mind. We depend on our own strength, forgetting that God has said he will guide us and be with us every step of the way.

When I was growing up I felt ordinary or average in all facets of my life. I had brown hair (neither blonde nor black), green eyes (neither blue nor brown), size 6½ shoe, 5'4" tall. Average, average, average. Average grades, average talents, average me. The first time I ever felt like I had done something extraordinary was when I gave birth to our son. At 9 pounds and 10 ounces, he was the biggest kid in the nursery. Other parents would gather at the nursery window and exclaim, "Look at *that* baby! Can you believe the size of that kid?" I called that big bundle of joy "Bruno" for the first few days of his life. He was astounding, and the name we had so carefully chosen for him before his birth just didn't seem spectacular enough. This kid was definitely *not* average.

I think that's how God feels about us. We are definitely *not* average in God's eyes. We are spectacular. *You* are spectacular. If we could see ourselves as God sees us, I think we would be amazed, humbled and ready to step up to whatever he calls us to do. We would never feel average again.

When we realize God wants to work with us to lead others to more fulfilling lives, we can take on the challenge boldly. We can do the things our hearts are telling us to do but that we feel inadequate to attempt.

Born leaders

Maybe you are a born leader and you know it. You can't wait to get out into the world every week and make your mark. You find opportunities in your work, your community, your home and your church to bless others by using your God-given gifts. You gladly step up to the task before you, whatever it may be, because you know God has given you abilities and expects you to use them to bless others.

If so, where is God calling you to lead today? Remember, even if you feel comfortable as a leader, you need to make sure you are not leading only in your own strength but in relationship with the one who guides you with eyes that see beyond the present.

Leading through influence

Leaders are not necessarily those people at the front of the parade. Although you may not have a title that identifies you as a leader in your workplace or community, you may be a leader because of your influence. Do people look to you to know what to do next? Do they value your opinion and ask for your input? Do they expect you to take the initiative when a decision needs to be made?

You don't have to be the smartest or most gifted individual, and you may not be at the top of the organizational chart, but if people look to you for help and listen to you to gain strength or wisdom, you are in a position to lead.

Andy Stanley says, "We have been called to be influencers. And the world is watching. Christ didn't commission us to become authorities so we could tell people how they ought to live. He called us to be influencers by the way we live, so people would want what we have."[78]

---

78   Andy Stanley, *Visioneering* (Sisters, Oregon: Multnomah Publishers, Inc., 1999), 190.

Constant assessment

When we are placed in roles of leadership, whether formally or informally, we need to constantly assess our own attitudes. We are called to servant leadership with Jesus as our example. If we're not careful we can let pride step in where humility is called for. True leaders are listeners. They spend time hearing what others need rather than assuming they already know.

Ken Blanchard and Phil Hodges, in their book, *Lead Like Jesus*, say, "The most persistent barrier to leading like Jesus is a heart motivated by self-interest."[79]

Do you truly have others' best interests in mind? Are you leading people to live better lives, encouraging them to use their own gifts and abilities? Are you leading in a positive direction?

When I was a teacher, I had a sixth grade class one year that was full of leaders. Unfortunately, every one of them was determined to lead the rest of the class down the wrong path. The other teachers and I were greatly concerned. "They are so strong, they'll either end up in prison or as CEOs of major corporations," we said *mostly* in jest. We were hoping for the CEO choice!

We can lead in positive or negative directions in our homes, work, churches, and communities.

In our homes we have the opportunity and responsibility to create havens of peace and comfort by showing strong, loving leadership. If you have young children, it may not seem very peaceful at times right now, but even in the noise of daily life, your children will know the security of being loved, as you provide for them. Even teenagers will recognize your values and

---

[79] Ken Blanchard and Phil Hodges, *Lead Like Jesus* (Nashville, Tennessee: Thomas Nelson Inc., 2005), 39.

will take note of them during those years when they seem to reject most of what you say. Your children's friends will also be influenced as they spend time in your home.

At work does gossip and ill-will permeate the atmosphere or do you and your co-workers encourage one another? You can make a difference by refusing to take part in the negativity. It is so easy to fall into a habit of griping and complaining and blaming others. You can be a silent beacon of good-will by refusing to contribute to that type of environment.

If you are in a position of authority, do employees look to you for wisdom and guidance or do they cower when you walk by, fearing an angry eruption? You can lead with true strength instead of through fear as many managers try to do.

"People who understand who they are, who know God and his power, can be people of great influence," say Henry and Richard Blackaby in *God in the Marketplace*. "They are not in bondage to other people's praise and affirmation. Their self-worth comes from their relationship with God. They are not enslaved to temptations that appeal to their pride. They don't put selfish interests above the well-being of their company, employees, and colleagues,"[80]

By finding the good in others and letting them know you value them as individuals even more than for their contributions, you spread the fragrance of God in the workplace.

"But thanks be to God, who always leads us in triumphal procession in Christ and through us spreads everywhere the fragrance of the knowledge of him. For we are to God the aroma of Christ among those who are being saved and those who are perishing." 2 Corinthians 2:14-15

---

80   Henry Blackaby and Richard Blackaby, *God in the Market Place* (Nashville, Tennessee: B & H Publishing Group, 2008), 23.

Our churches are great places to exhibit positive leadership. You've probably known men and women who have created havoc in churches by gossiping, criticizing the preacher, or complaining endlessly. We can influence for good by showing integrity under all circumstances. We can be encouragers, using uplifting words instead of complaints. Praying for our church leaders and letting them know we are doing so is a great gift to them.

Answering God's call completely

When we first answer 'yes' to God's call and yield to him with complete obedience, we may wonder, *Is God calling me to fulltime Christian service in ministry of some kind?* That's an important question to ask. You very well may be called to a vocation within the church or in some capacity as a minister or missionary. However, Christian leaders are needed in every aspect of life—not only within a Christian setting. Where has God called you to be his representative? Medicine, education, sales, law, art, music, business, entrepreneurship? We do need to commit to fulltime Christian service, because we are Christians 24/7, but that service may take place in the secular world.

What an opportunity you have to model the love of God in schools, corporations, public institutions, politics or other public areas. If you are a Christian you are representing the faith, whether you realize it or not. Indeed, you may have as much opportunity in the workplace to share your life and bless others as you would if you were seen as a "professional Christian"—a clergy person.

In the business world and in your community activities, you can make a difference in the lives of those around you who may have never entered the doors of a church. This reality is apparent more and more in today's society. Some of your workmates and neighbors may be antagonistic toward Christianity because of past hurts, while others simply have not grown up with Christian influences and may be completely unaware of what it's really all about. Your influence is needed today more than ever to model Christ's love. This calls for commitment, not perfection. Your true character will be apparent to those working with you day after day. You don't have to create a Christian image; your authentic self will be enough if you are living a Christ-filled life. God uses us in spite of our failures, just as he did those leaders mentioned in the Bible.

Maybe your area of expertise is in art, drama, film, music or some other creative endeavor. Opportunities abound to influence for good in those spheres of influence.

Makoto Fujimura, the New York artist mentioned in Chapter Six, understands. "Artists are leaders simply because we are in the 'enterprise of persuasion,'…with that comes great responsibility…to use that persuasive influence to create the 'world that ought to be.'"[81]

On the other hand, you may very well be called to the ministry as a vocation. If so, you will want to take advantage of the best training available to you. Don't worry about how you will be able to do this, just be faithful to God's calling and pray for opportunities to open up for you.

This is an exciting time to be a woman in ministry professionally. There are so many different areas of ministry available to us—some especially suited to women. How much better to have a caring woman to minister to women and children who

---

81   Makoto Fujimura, *Christianity Today*, "Re-Imagining Reality" (September 2008), 31.

have been abused or neglected—one to whom the injured can talk more easily.

Many barriers have come down, allowing women to use their God-given gifts in ways not always open to previous generations of women. You who are already in ministry can mentor and encourage those who come after you. You who enter the profession today will take the hand of one who has gone before you and reach back to one who comes later, creating a chain of hope and help. Instead of competition, we join with both men and women to further the kingdom work God calls us to.

Whether as a lay person or clergy, we are all called to be servant leaders. Each place is equally important. No honorable profession is more important than another on God's list. Together we work to bear burdens and point wanderers toward home.

You are called to lead and to lead wisely.

"Those who are wise will shine like the brightness of the heavens, and those who lead many to righteousness, like the stars for ever and ever." Daniel 12:3

We may be called to go beyond the boundaries of comfort in reaching out to others who need healing of heart and soul. Our differences could be economical, social, or even age-related.

Ken Blanchard and Phil Hodges remind us, "Jesus spent significant time interacting in positive ways with people who disagreed with Him. He did not isolate Himself from those who disagreed; He embraced those who disagreed. He did not change His message to gain approval, but He continued to love those who did not accept His message."[82]

---

82   Ken Blanchard and Phil Hodges, 30.

You don't need to be a part of a particular generational group to be able to minister to the people in that age bracket. You may be a young woman who is called to work with older, retired people or you may be an older person who is called to mentor younger women. When working with people outside of our own demographic, it helps to understand something about our differences.

A young minister recently joined the staff at our church. He is smart, knowledgeable, just finished his Ph.D. in theology and is ornamented with piercings and tattoos. Now since this church is rather conventional in most ways, this new minister raised some eyebrows when he was brought on board. I'm fascinated by his ministry. He didn't give up his own identity when he became a minister. Instead, God uses his unique personality to reach others. His calling is to those of his generation who may have never entered the doors of a church. He fits right in with those to whom he ministers.

True Christian leadership means leading others to the hope of the world by meeting them where they are and loving them as God loves them.

Your turn to serve
What are your greatest strengths? If you've been journaling, look through your entries at your personality type, your spiritual gifts and the things that bring you immense joy. Where can these attributes be used to the greatest degree in leading others? Are you a problem-solver? A peacemaker? Do you excel at teaching others what you know? Do you have the gift of service, reaching out to others or making sure the job gets done wherever you are? Perhaps you have the gift of hospitality and use that to make others feel welcome and appreciated.

Does your very presence brighten a room when you enter? Or are you meticulous in details, assuring that nothing is forgotten? All of these various abilities meet needs in different ways.

Where is God calling you to lead? How can you guide and challenge others to grow and become their best? What experiences have you had that can comfort someone going through a tough time?

"But in your hearts set apart Christ as Lord. Always be prepared to give an answer to everyone who asks you to give the reason for the hope that you have. But do this with gentleness and respect" (1 Peter 3:15)

Journey of a lifetime

When we embrace the journey to become the persons God created us to be, by doing the hard work of getting to know ourselves and committing our lives to the path God would have us walk, we begin to live authentically. We are able to drop the façades that have kept us from being all God had in mind for us from the beginning. We give up our striving and relax in the arms of the one who loves us unconditionally. In turn, we learn to love others as God loves us.

Christian speaker and singer Janet Birkey sums it up like this:

> I think I am beginning to get a glimpse of real authenticity. We all want to be the new, plush, luxurious Velveteen Rabbit, but it really seems that our true selves and value come only after the 'pretty'

has been loved off of us by a Father who knew what we were supposed to look like all along. Here's to going bald and being loved to death by the One who has loved us before time.[83]

The journey goes on for a lifetime. We may find it exhilarating, invigorating, perplexing or daunting, but it will never be boring, if we remain teachable. There's always more to learn about God, ourselves and how we can be used to bless others.

Author Nancy Ortberg, puts it all in perspective as she tells of seeing the stage production *Les Miserables* with her husband John:

> Toward the end of the play, as the hero, Jean Valjean, is near death, he sings to his adopted daughter, Cosette, 'To love another person is to see the face of God.'
>
> As I watched the scene, tears began streaming down my face. "That's one of the truest and most beautiful phrases I've ever heard," I told John. "Why didn't God make that a verse in the Bible?"
>
> A few weeks later, John said, "I want to read you something."
>
> He opened his Bible to Genesis 33 and read the words of Jacob, reunited with Esau after having been estranged for a long time: "For to see your face is like seeing the face of God" (verse 10).[84]

---

83   Janet Birkey, personal correspondence with the author.
84   Nancy Ortberg, *Today's Christian Woman*, "When Devos Don't Work" (September/October, 2008), 28.

The Authentic You: Becoming the Woman You Were Created to Be

As we grow into the likeness of Jesus, we are able to show a hurting world that each of us can be more than we thought we could be, because of the love of our Creator.

We are called to daily, lovingly proclaim that message. Each of us is invited to make a difference in the world. What an awesome responsibility. What an amazing privilege.

I hope you will accept the invitation to live this life of abundance. After walking boldly with Jesus for a time and sharing his marvelous love with those around you, you will indeed reflect the face of God.

When that happens, there will be no doubt that you have become the authentic you—the woman God created you to be.

* * *

Now to him who is able to do immeasurably more than all we ask or imagine, according to his power that is at work within us, to him be glory in the church and in Christ Jesus throughout all generations, for ever and ever! Amen. (Ephesians 3:20-21)

ACTION STEPS:

1. Who is in your sphere of influence: family, co-workers, church friends, community members?
2. How is God calling you to lead in the areas where you live your daily life?
3. What are the special gifts, talents, interests, or abilities you have that can be used to influence other people to live fully?
4. Do you feel God's nudging to break out of your comfort zone and do something that would be impossible without God's help?
5. Are you thinking big enough and dreaming big enough?
6. Ask God to show you where you need to lead as an authentic woman of God, created to be God's representative to a hurting world!

A message from the Author—

Dear Friend,

I've shared some of my life story with you, and I pray that it has been helpful. I would love to hear your story and how this book may have impacted your life.

Please feel free to contact me by email at: **AuthenticYou@AnitaCLee.com** and let me know how God is working in your life.

Also, if you are interested in having me speak to your group or if you want information about life coaching with me, see my website, **www.AnitaCLee.com** or email me at **AuthenticYou@AnitaCLee.com**.

I wish you Godspeed on your journey as you continue to grow and become the woman you were created to be.

Abundant blessings,
Anita C. Lee

A percentage of the proceeds of this book goes to World Vision International to help women around the world create better lives for their families.
www.worldvision.org

About the Author:

Anita C. Lee is a personal life coach, speaker, and CEO of Authentic Success, LLC. She helps her clients become the women they were created to be, empowering them to break through their fears and hesitancy to soar, to become authentically successful entrepreneurs, mothers, community and church leaders, and business professionals.

Through personal life coaching, speaking, seminars and writing opportunities, Anita encourages women to boldly step out of their comfort zones and make positive differences in the world, using their God-given gifts and abilities.

Anita holds an MA in education, is a certified life coach through Coach Training Alliance, and is a Certified Personality Trainer through CLASSeminars.

Anita lives in Albuquerque, NM, where she enjoys activities with her family (including tea parties with the Grand Princesses), choral music and travel. She can be contacted through her website at www.AnitaCLee.com.

Made in the USA
Charleston, SC
20 December 2010